Were You at
the Game?

Were You at the Game?

the story of Jimmy Sanderson
and the Radio Clyde football phone-in

MICHAEL SANDERSON
with Paul Cooney

ARGYLL✣PUBLISHING

© Michael Sanderson 2007

First published in 2007
Argyll Publishing
Glendaruel
Argyll PA22 3AE
Scotland
www.argyllpublishing.com

The right of Michael Sanderson to be identified as the author
of this work has been asserted by him in accordance with the
Copyright, Designs and Patents Act of 1988.

British Library Cataloguing-in-Publication Data.
A catalogue record for this book is available from
the British Library.

ISBN 978 1 906134 06 8

Printing: Bell & Bain Ltd, Glasgow

This book is dedicated to the memory of my father, and to callers and listeners of football phone-ins everywhere, past and present, here and 'in spirit'.

"Only a fool would predict a result for this match.
I go for a draw."

Hugh Taylor, Scottish sports journalist, 1970s

Contents

Acknowledgements   9

Foreword by Richard Park   11

Introduction   13

Chapter 1   Warming Up   23

Chapter 2   Argentina 1978   38

Chapter 3   The Emergence of The New Firm   50

Chapter 4   Crisis – What Crisis?   61

Chapter 5   Tribute to Jock Stein   73

Chapter 6   Crossing Swords   75

Chapter 7   1986 – Sanderson's Finale   87

Chapter 8   The Show Must Go On   94

References   101

Appendix   103

Jimmy Sanderson in the late 1960s with trademark cigar

Acknowledgements

The starting point for writing this book followed a visit to the Scottish Football Museum at Hampden Park with my wife Bernadette in 2005. One of the main exhibits featured Radio Clyde, and it was here that I listened once again to the very familiar voice of my late father, eighteen years after his death in December 1986. The written material explaining who he was in Scottish football used the term 'legendary' before his name, and my wife turned to me and said, "If he is legendary, then why isn't there a book about him?"

I visited Paul Cooney at Radio Clyde shortly after, and we discussed the idea of a book for charity to commemorate my father's life as a sports journalist. As he is best remembered for his Radio Clyde 'Super-Scoreboard' contributions, back in the days when Richard Park, Dougie Donnelly, 'Tiger' Tim Stevens, Dave Marshall and Paul Coia were all key members of the Radio Clyde team (along with a youthful Paul Cooney); it seemed appropriate that my father's time at Radio Clyde should be a main focus of the book.

My father's colleague of many years, the late Jim

Rodger, had passed old press cuttings to my mother covering some of the main events in Scottish football up until the mid-1980s that my father had reported on. These were swiftly retrieved from my mother's loft, and I thank her for safeguarding this material which would be a 'gold-mine' when it came to sitting down and planning this book.

I have found in life that you never get the best results without the help of family and friends. My love and thanks go to my wife Bernadette; mother Sheila; sister Valerie and cousin Lesley for their encouragement as the book gradually took shape.

I am fortunate in that there are a number of people whom I can always rely on for their friendship and support, and who I spent hours with in discussions over different aspects of this book. My thanks go to David Levinson, James Johnston, Russell Campbell, John Preston, Ian 'Grouch' Margetts, Simon Rao, Jim Clark and Meg Clark.

Thanks also go to colleagues of my father from past years: Rodger Baillie, Jimmy Findlay and Dick Currie; who all provided personal insights from years ago; and to Mary Hamilton for providing a photo from my father's time at the *Scottish Daily Express*. I am also indebted to Derek Rodger of Argyll Publishing for his advice and expertise.

Lastly my sincere thanks go to the staff who searched the archives at Radio Clyde, to the staff at the Mitchell library, Glasgow, and the staff at the Scottish Football Museum at Hampden Park.

Michael Sanderson
June 2007

Foreword

A book about Jimmy Sanderson is a great idea as he deserves to be recognised. His achievements in broadcasting and journalism are legendary

Those first Radio Clyde football phone-in programmes were the original reality show. They mixed tension and humour with passion and dedication and were the original football phone-in show. No other programme on radio ever came close to matching them.

Jimmy had a sense of timing normally given to a thespian and his command of the English language smacked of the days when our language was a thing of beauty.

Whether dressed in his best or shivering under a blanket in the front row of the stand at places like Hamilton's Douglas Park, he was a consummate professional.

James Sanderson was an inspiration to me and our seven year stint together represented some of the best days I ever had. Never a dull moment and much to treasure. I learned a lot from him.

Richard Park

James Sanderson with Kilmarnock players including Tommy McLean (centre) on a tour of Rhodesia, 1970

With Scottish football journalists in Spain 1967/68 (l to r) Willie Waddell, John McKenzie, Davie White (then Rangers manager), Drew Rennie, Hugh Taylor and James Sanderson

Introduction

R ichard Park: "Ah, hello caller, you're through now."

Caller 1: "Hello."

James Sanderson: "Yes hello, James Sanderson here, what's your question?"

Caller 1: "Mr Sanderson, eh. . . , my question's this. See me and the . . . oh by the way, it's good to have you back Mr Sanderson!"

James Sanderson: "Well that's very kind of you."

Caller 1: "See me and the boys were having a wee discussion, and we wanted to know what you think about. . . , see what it is. . . , is eh. . . , I mean I don't know the boy okay?. . . "

James Sanderson: "Uh-huh."

Caller 1: "But basically. . . , what it is, right, it's . . . 'em. . . , I mean, . . . it's Cammy Fraser. . . , I'd like to know what you think of that?"

James Sanderson: "Do you mind if I ask *you* a question?"

Caller 1: "What is it Mr. Sanderson?"

James Sanderson: "Were you **at** the game today?"

Caller 1: "No, no I wasn't."

James Sanderson: "Ah, well you see . . . "

Caller 1: "I'm sorry Mr Sanderson, I couldnae go the day. . . I was at the wife's funeral, and I had my tranny . . . I had my tranny with me though, and I listened to your commentary, and I'd just like to say, I think you and Richard did a great job."

James Sanderson: "Well thanks very much, but even so, how long can a funeral take? Surely you could have made it along for the second half at least?"

Caller 1: "Well you see, I'm unemployed Mr Sanderson, I cannae really afford to go. . ."

James Sanderson: "No, no I'm sorry, I'm sorry – that's just not good enough! You must have some money coming to you if your wife's just died. Now I really think you should be making a bit more of an effort here!"

Caller 1: "Well, you see Mr Sanderson, I've got the kids to look after. . . "

James Sanderson: "Ah now, that's just pure bunkum, to use a favourite expression of mine. Can't they be put into care for one day a week? You see, we're talking at cross purposes here, caller. My job is to get people into games. I want bottoms on seats! I want your bottom, caller! I mean I've had Dougie Donnelly's bottom before this, and I've had Richard Park's bottom. . . "

Richard Park: "Yes, um you certainly have James, um. . .

have you not, but before we go too deeply into my bottom, I want to bring in your second caller. . . Hello caller, you're through to James Sanderson."

Caller 2: "Hello, hello James?"

James Sanderson: "Yes sir?"

Caller 2: "James, I'd like to take issue with you on something you said on radio this afternoon."

James Sanderson: "Oh, oh you would, would you. . . ?"

Caller 2: "Yes, you described a Brian McClair goal as: '. . . unequivocal in its execution'."

James Sanderson: "That's correct, that's correct. And what if I did. . . ?"

Caller 2: "Well, I feel perhaps you confused the categorical affirmative tense with the recurrent subjunctive here. I mean the term you actually should have used is irrefragable!"

James Sanderson: "Ah now, now just a moment! I think. . . I think that's quite refulgent of you to say so, if you don't mind me . . . "

Caller 2: "Hmm."

James Sanderson: "No, no, no just a moment, just a moment; . . . are you . . . are you accusing me of mendacity?"

Caller 2: "Well, I'm afraid I am James, and even verbosity!"

James Sanderson: "Well that is sheer poppy-cock, that is nothing but outright bunkum and balderdash!"

Caller 2: "Now come on, that's not fair James; I mean you're making words up now . . ."

James Sanderson: "I beg your pardon! Well, we'll have to agree to differ there, caller. I am irrevocable in my contention and unequivocal. And, by the way, I have said this to Brian McClair's face, by the way. . . unequivocal was the corroborative definitive eh. . . eh. . . description of his goal."

Caller 2: "Well you see James, I lecture at Glasgow University in English language. Its usage . . ."

James Sanderson: "Excuse me, excuse me! Don't flash your credentials at me sir! I. . . I. . . I've travelled the world with Scotland. I have travelled alongside Stein, Busby, Shankly. I've showered with Kenny Dalglish, so don't bandy words with me. And anyway, as I've said before, and I've said this a good while, I don't like. . . I don't like to intellectualise unnecessarily about football. Now if you don't mind, caller, what is your question?"

Caller 2: "My, my question, oh yes, well I'd like to ask you this. Cammy Fraser, what do you think about that then?"

Sound of James Sanderson angrily slamming the phone down.

> Parody of Radio Clyde Football Open Line (1986):
> 'Only an Excuse' Naked Radio, BBC

***

The phrase 'Were you at the game?' became synonymous with the Radio Clyde football phone-in of the early to mid-1980s. The phone-in, Clyde Super-Scoreboard, was hosted by Richard Park, a talented disc jockey and broadcaster who in later years would move to Capital Radio in London, and then became famous for his involvement in the BBC talent show 'Fame Academy'. Also present on the team was Paul Cooney, who would rise to become Managing Director of Radio Clyde.

The expertise on the programme was provided by James Sanderson, nick-named 'Solly' by fellow journalists (or sometimes 'Hans Christian'), and who had travelled the world as a sports journalist as both a boxing and football writer. He had seen Cassius Clay win the light-heavyweight gold medal at the Olympic Games in Rome in 1960, and had followed the exploits of Walter McGowan, Ken Buchanan and Jim Watt as professional world boxing champions, as well as the amateur exploits of Dick McTaggart at Olympic level in 1956 winning gold at lightweight. He had even been appointed as one of the judges at McGowan's 1966 world title defence in Bangkok, where McGowan was stopped on a cut.

Likewise, he had witnessed many an Old Firm tussle, admiring the skills of those such as Jim Baxter and Jimmy Johnstone. He had written about some of the best players ever to have pulled on a Scotland shirt, including Denis Law and Kenny Dalglish. He witnessed European Cup glory for Celtic in Lisbon in 1967; Cup Winners' Cup success for Rangers in 1972 in Barcelona, Spain; and was with Aberdeen when they defeated Real Madrid in Gothenburg, Sweden in 1983 in the Cup Winners' Cup final. He had also followed the fortunes of the Scottish national team since before the 1958 World Cup campaign, (again in Sweden). Alongside colleagues such as Alex Cameron, Hugh Taylor and Jim Rodger, they had covered the highs and lows of Scottish sport (the greatest low being present at the Ibrox disaster at the end of the Ne'erday game in January 1971, where the bodies were laid out on the pitch).

Sanderson had held a plum job as chief sportswriter for the *Scottish Daily Express* for nearly twenty years, with a column entitled 'The Sanderson Slant', but in 1974 the *Scottish Daily Express* office located at Albion Street in Glasgow was closed, with the staff being made redundant. In the aftermath, he was preparing to emigrate with his family to New Zealand to start a new life, having been impressed by what he saw of the country when covering the 1974 Commonwealth Games in Christchurch (one of his last *Express* assignments).

However, MGN-Mirror Group Newspapers (based in Glasgow's Anderston Quay) – offered him a job in a bid to launch the *Daily Mirror* in Scotland. The initial idea was to build up significantly the circulation of the *Daily Mirror* north of the border. At that time it was already the biggest selling tabloid in England along with *The Sun*. However, the promises never materialised as management back-tracked over the launch. There was a reason for this, as the *Daily Mirror's* sister paper the *Daily Record* was the best-selling tabloid in Scotland, and it was feared that boosting *Mirror* sales would merely cannibalise sales from the *Daily Record*, and effectively score an own goal.

Having been a successful sports-writer all his life, the *Mirror* job proved frustrating. Circulation in Scotland was low, the *Record* would not allow him to jump ship and write for them, and he suffered the ignominy of being transferred to a tiny room. Things were looking bleak, but world-cup failure in Argentina in 1978 by the Scotland national team, and the debate over whether Ally MacLeod as Scottish team manager should resign, were to act as a catalyst that would effectively save Sanderson's journalistic career, as well as launch the formula for a new and exciting concept: the football phone-in.

Radio Clyde had the advantage of a large west of Scotland following, the vast majority either supporting Celtic or Rangers. This translated well into audiences, as both sets of supporters would listen, even if the live game coverage was not directly involving their team (the conditions imposed on radio coverage allowed transmission of the last five minutes of the first half, and the whole of the second half for live commentary). Thus, if the Old Firm derby was aired then both sets of supporters could listen and cheer on their team. If Celtic were playing Aberdeen, for example, the Celtic supporters would listen and follow their team, whereas Rangers supporters would also listen, desperately hoping to hear that Celtic would suffer defeat. And vice-versa. Radio Clyde's strategy was simple, each week cover one of the Old Firm sides, and you were guaranteed a big audience (but make sure that you give equal coverage of number of league games played by the Old Firm!).

The Old Firm bias meant that, as a commercial radio station, the number of listeners remained high for Radio Clyde's Super-Scoreboard, and premium advertising rates could be charged for a slot on a Saturday afternoon. In short, it was box office.

Sanderson's involvement came by chance. Radio Clyde

had an established discussion/debate programme that occurred every Sunday mid-morning, known as the 'Sunday Talk-in'. Here relevant topics were debated such as 'Should hanging be re-introduced in the UK?' Listeners were invited to call in to the live programme and air their views. Following the World Cup debacle in Argentina, where Scotland had gone having been triumphantly waved off at a special ceremony at Hampden Park, high hopes had been replaced by humiliation. A defeat to Peru, a draw with Iran, and the unlikely climax of a 'near miss' towards qualification to the latter tournament stages against Holland (the highlight being the 'play-ground' goal scored by Archie Gemmill), had meant that the Scottish public was somewhat divided at the time as to the fate of Ally MacLeod.

Radio Clyde decided to host a Sunday phone-in debate entitled 'Ally MacLeod – Stay or Go?' They required the services of a seasoned journalist willing to give an opinion and who had witnessed events first hand in Argentina. Sanderson was not first choice, and in fact only featured because he had answered the phone that Sunday morning at 7am, as frantic Radio Clyde staff desperately phoned around for a replacement for the journalist who had called off sick (they were not divulging who it was). In fact Sanderson was a good choice, as he had written some of the finest copy of his career on the Argentina expedition. He had managed to gain access to some of the best scoops, including the failure of a drug test by Willie Johnston. He was one of the few journalists to travel in the same plane with the Scotland team, and so the *Mirror* had benefited from the dramas that had unfolded.

Another factor was also going to be unveiled. Sanderson had a distinctive high nasal voice, perfect for the medium of radio, and certainly ripe to be mimicked. The voice projected his charisma and strong personality, and his grammar school education was evident in his extensive vocabulary – dull this was not! As the programme commenced, he was asked by the anchorman to declare his opinion as to Ally Macleod's continued tenure. Sanderson's reply was characteristically forthright. "MacLeod should resign this instant. Argentina has been an unmitigated disaster. He should go now!"

The switchboard red lights (indicating callers queuing) instantaneously gave off an angry glow; the lines were jammed. The journey of discovery had started.

James Sanderson (front row, third from left) doing National Service at West Kirkby Training Camp, 1947. While in the Royal Air Force, he competed as an amateur boxer in the flyweight and bantamweight divisions

Chapter One: Warming Up

James Millar Sanderson was born into a working-class family in Glasgow on March 25th, 1929. His father Alex was a baker and wedding-cake confectioner, his mother Kitty had suffered from rheumatic fever and gave birth to three children. James was the eldest child, with two sisters, Doreen and Sheila. All inherited health problems relating to heart conditions with high blood pressure, and like their parents, none would reach the age of sixty years old.

The family home was in Riddrie, on Glasgow's East side, but with the outbreak of World War II, the family was evacuated to Dunoon. This was to be beneficial to the eldest son James, as he would attend Dunoon Grammar school, excelling in English, Latin and History. James then started a journalistic career as an apprentice on the *Evening News* in Glasgow as a copy boy, acting as a gofer and taking the copy written by journalists to the print-room, where the newspaper copy was arranged by compositors using lead type. Other duties as a copy boy included telephoning the copy by dictating the reports. He knew sports journalism was for him when in 1947 he was given the responsibility to telephone the copy of the Great Britain v Europe football match, where the great Billy Steel played a blinder.

However, his apprenticeship was interrupted with the small matter of National Service to be served in 1947. James had been in the Air Training Corps (ATC), and had won a Scottish Command ATC boxing title at flyweight in Edinburgh. He then competed at the ATC British Championship semi-finals in Leeds. At only 5 feet 3 inches many sports would be unsuitable for his stature, but not boxing, as with its weight categories he could take forward his advantage of being very strong for his size. He would later be told at his RAF medical as he enlisted for National Service that his broad shoulders were that of a man of 5 feet 10 inches. He volunteered for the Royal Air Force, and was sent to a base in England called White Waltham. Here he would meet at aged eighteen his future wife Sheila, a Lancashire girl who had volunteered at 18 years old as a WRAF to escape a life of poverty in Salford.

The RAF was keen to have him and he was immediately seconded to the RAF boxing team. This was a smart move, as much of the time was devoted to training. The members of the boxing team benefited from authorised leave after contests as a reward for their efforts, as well as receiving special high protein diets (mostly steak).

There was a price to be paid, however, as rivalry between RAF stations meant that boxing evenings were regularly held in empty hangars. Officers could only box against fellow officers; there was no question of mixing the ranks in the ring. Large crowds of RAF servicemen attended these events, specially put on to alleviate boredom in the evenings and help boost morale in the forces. Sanderson was small, fast and good. He won an RAF Reserve Inter-Station Championship at Flyweight in 1947, then moved up to Bantamweight in January 1948, taking part in the

Inter-Command Championships at RAF Colerne.

The well-respected football commentator Archie MacPherson would also comment on Sanderson's pugilistic abilities (albeit many years later, and not in a boxing ring) in his book *Jock Stein* (2005), where he related the tale of a fracas involving Sanderson and an English journalist, Peter Lorenzo, after Celtic had played Racing Club of Argentina for the world club championship in November 1967. There had been animosity from the English press who begrudged Celtic's success earlier in Lisbon that year, and had considered that Celtic had been lucky. MacPherson writes:

> One such was Peter Lorenzo, an English journalist and broadcaster who was known to have given Celtic some savaging in his reports and who was upbraided by an equally famous Scottish journalist James Sanderson, or 'Solly' as he was generally known, in the airport lounge before flying home from Montevideo when there was a delay for two hours because of fog. In keeping with the mayhem of the previous day, Solly, who would have entered the boxing ring as a bantamweight, decided to defend Celtic's honour against the heavyweight Lorenzo's bad mouthing by delivering him a swift right hook to the chin, which floored the Englishman. Although apologies were made for this misconduct, by other journalists, Solly had acted as many of his colleagues had felt like doing, though they had opted to uphold that old adage that the pen is mightier than the sword. (page 184)

Back in 1949, Sanderson had enjoyed his two years national service in the RAF, and was tempted to sign up for a longer stint. However, he was keen to re-embark on his journalistic career, and returned to Civvy Street where he took several jobs in Manchester (to be near his future wife Sheila), including the *Daily Graphic* and the *Chronicle*. The precarious nature of being a newspaper journalist was brought home to him when one of the Manchester papers employing him went bust, the staff somewhat belatedly discovering this fact from a notice that was pinned inside the lift that was used for access to the offices. It was 1951, and time to return home to Glasgow.

A job with the *Daily Record* in the early 1950s consisted of covering junior football matches, such as clubs like Pollok Juniors, Petershill and Dennistoun Waverly. Part of the job involved commandeering the local telephone kiosk so that a match report could be delivered back to the office copy-takers. Also part of the contract was covering boxing at venues such as the Grove Stadium in Glasgow. He learned the ropes of sports newspaper journalism.

Earlier in his career he had done a stint on the news-desk of one of the Manchester papers, and had been horrified when he had been tasked to go to the door of the family where a young girl had died in a road accident. The newspaper required him to ask the mother for a recent photograph of the deceased to print as part of the tragic story. This had convinced him that sports reporting would be a preferred option, although the Busby Babes Munich air disaster in the 1950s, and the Ibrox disaster of 1971, would bring home the point that, in life, tragedy did not preclude sport.

Sanderson's journalistic career blossomed ironically not so much due to football, but because of his first love, the sport of boxing. This would be the passage to building up expertise and make his early career. His knowledge of boxing was especially good because he had been a successful amateur. He understood the tactics of boxing. 'Kill the body and you kill the head.' 'Box a fighter and fight a boxer.' He knew the difference between a jab, hook, cross and uppercut; as well as orthodox and southpaw. He understood the requirement for intensive training in the gym, good diet, road-work and stamina. That good footwork and being able to box defensively, as well as the skill of in-fighting, were all skills to be honed to master the noble art.

He also knew that boxing was a game for those blessed with the ability to punch hard. He often cited the quote of Sugar Ray Robinson, who had explained that when starting out as an amateur he would throw a punch, and the opponent would simply 'fall down'. It also helped if you did not succumb to cuts, a sure way for any professional not to last 'the distance' (Henry Cooper being a fine example of 'a bleeder').

When the *Record's* Elky Clark, an excellent professional flyweight who had fought for a world title, retired as the *Record's* boxing writer, Sanderson filled the void. He would cover both boxing and football, but most of the more glamorous assignments, involving world travel, would be for boxing title fights he was sent to cover. As a sports writer his boxing writing attracted the attentions of rival newspapers, and he was snapped up by the *Scottish Daily Express* in the mid-1950s, again with a remit to cover boxing and football. Boxing was still in its hey-day, with big fights still requiring the use of football grounds as venues due to the popularity of the sport. In the future, this popularity would wane.

The move to the *Scottish Daily Express* proved successful.

On the footballing front he was sent to cover the Scottish national team's world cup exploits in 1958. It was there that he first saw the majestic skills of a young Brazilian called Pele. He would in later years go on to cover Scotland's campaigns in West Germany in 1974, Argentina in 1978, Spain in 1982; but not Mexico 1986 (he was advised not to travel by medical staff following a heart attack in December 1985).

He rated Pele, Beckenbauer and Cruyff as the best he had ever seen; with George Best the finest UK player. The match he rated the best he had ever seen was Real Madrid versus Eintracht Frankfurt, the 1960 European Cup Final played at Hampden Park, where Real Madrid won the game 7-3. Rangers had reached the semi-final stage of the European Cup for season 1959-60, but suffered two heavy defeats to Eintracht Frankfurt, losing 6-1 and 6-3 as Eintracht progressed to the Hampden Final.

From the mid-1950s, Sanderson would go on countless sojourns with Scottish clubs as they travelled abroad for European fixtures, following the fortunes of clubs including Celtic, Rangers, Aberdeen, Dundee, Dundee United, Dunfermline, Kilmarnock and Hibs. In the 1960s football highlights not involving the Old Firm that Sanderson witnessed included Dundee in a European Cup semi-final in 1963, losing to AC Milan 5-2 on aggregate (AC Milan then went on to defeat Benfica 2-1 in the Final at Wembley). In the Fairs Cup, Hibernian and Kilmarnock also did well. Hibernian reached the semi-final of the Fairs Cup in 1961, losing to Roma. In 1967 Kilmarnock also reached the semi-final of the Fairs Cup, losing to Leeds United. Dunfermline reached the semi-final of the Cup Winners' Cup in 1969, but lost to eventual winners Slovan Bratislava.

He was also in Europe with Partick Thistle and Clyde, and went on a pre-season tour with Kilmarnock to Rhodesia in 1970 (of which both Tommy McLean who would later join Rangers, and Ally Hunter who would keep goal for Scotland against Czechoslovakia in 1973, were members of the Kilmarnock squad). During the Rhodesian tour, Sanderson was formally introduced to Ian Smith, then the prime minister of a country that practised apartheid. All was pleasant until a discussion between the two men concerning the sport of boxing turned into a heated clash over the possibility of the emergence of a 'white hope' heavyweight champion. The meeting was then abruptly adjourned – they would have to agree to differ!

Another story of Sanderson's combative nature is told by Alan Davidson of the *Evening Times*. He reports the outcome of. . .

> . . . a confrontation between James 'Solly' Sanderson and the then Rangers manager Willie Waddell. 'Solly' was a dapper little man with a unique style who had worked on many newspapers and was a renowned broadcaster. He also had a fiery temperament and when Waddell poked a finger at him over a piece he had written he responded from a height of some five feet four inches: "You and your views are a matter of total irrelevance to me. Goodbye".
>
> (*Evening Times*, 13th January, 2004)

*

With the *Scottish Daily Express*, and as a member of the Boxing Writers' Association, Sanderson was covering European and World title fights. He did not just cover professional boxing, but amateur boxing also. He saw Jim Watt knock out John Stracey in under a minute at the ABA semi-finals in 1968, and would travel with the Scottish amateur boxing team to international tournaments. After Dick McTaggart won Olympic gold at lightweight in 1956, Sanderson was asked by professional promoters to act as a 'go-between' to see if McTaggart could be persuaded to join the paid ranks. Sanderson was instructed to offer a considerable cash incentive. He was struck by McTaggart's strength of character, and admired his resolve. McTaggart would not be turning professional.

For Scotland, it was the smaller men that delivered success in what is known as 'the hardest game'. Peter Keenan was a popular champion, who drew big crowds for his contests. On the world stage, Walter McGowan had become world flyweight champion in 1966. Sanderson was the only Scottish journalist to be sent to cover McGowan's ill-fated title fight in Bangkok against Chartchai Chioni which took place on December 30th 1966. McGowan's camp was unhappy as it feared that fair play may not be seen to be observed, and arguments from both camps led to an unsavoury atmosphere in the heat of the Far East. Mistrust led to concerns over the judging of the contest. McGowan's father requested that Sanderson be appointed a judge for the fight. In an interview with Roddy Forsyth in *Scottish Field* in early 1986, Sanderson reminisced on events:

> Yes, it was hot stuff from the Orient. There were all
> sorts of complications surrounding the fight. Joe
> Gans, Walter's father, asked me to be a judge, and I

accepted. Soon after, we went to a reception with members of the military junta which ruled Thailand.

One of the generals said to me: 'You'll be presented to the King and Queen of Thailand after Chioni wins the title.'

I said: 'Excuse me – IF he wins the title.'

There was a long silence and nobody spoke to me again. I never got my fee for acting as a judge and I left the country in rather a bad odour.

In the event the fight never got to the judges' scorecards. McGowan was stopped because of a bad cut on the nose in the ninth round (McGowan also lost a rematch to the same opponent in 1967). However, Sanderson learned that there was an even more brutal sport than the noble art. He was taken to see an evening of Thai Boxing during his visit to Bangkok, where he witnessed the vast majority of the evening's losers leaving the ring on a stretcher.

The next Scottish fighter for Sanderson to report on for world championship honours was Ken Buchanan, who won the world lightweight title from Ismael Laguna in San Juan, Puerto Rico back in 1970. Nearly two years later Sanderson was in New York with his friend and colleague Dick Currie, to cover the Madison Square Garden world title event of Buchanan and a certain Roberto Duran in 1972, which Duran won in controversial circumstances with a stoppage late in the fight. Dick Currie was the *Daily Record* boxing writer, and had been an excellent international amateur, winning Commonwealth Gold at flyweight in 1954 in Vancouver, Canada. Both Sanderson and Currie arrived at their New York hotel, and decided it was a nice evening to take a stroll in Central Park. Ten minutes into the walk a NYPD police car drew up beside them. It transpired that they were strolling into dangerous territory, and were ordered into the police car and given a lift back to the hotel, where they walked through the lobby rather sheepishly. "You're obviously not New Yorkers," the police officer had remarked. "At this time of night is when the crazies come out!"

Following on from Buchanan, it was the turn of Jim Watt. In the late 1960s Sanderson had considered Watt a very good amateur. He had reported on Watt as a Scottish international for the *Scottish Daily Express* in January 1968:

> Scotland went down 4-3 in an injury-shortened match here in Aalborg tonight after the Danes had astonishingly banned lightweight Jim Watt from boxing against them. . . because he is too good! Watt, eighteen-year-old Glasgow apprentice electrician and Western District champion, was ready to fight Jutland's Per Falk Christensen in what would have been the eighth bout of the match. But the Danes, who had seen Watt smash his way to a two-minute win in what was his international debut in Copenhagen two nights ago, banned him. Their team manager said: "Our boxer is not good enough to meet Watt. He could be badly hurt and we will not permit the match."
>
> Source – *Watt's My Name,* 1981, (pp136-137)

Sanderson was also present at the Watt v Buchanan British lightweight title fight held at the St. Andrew's Sporting Club, Glasgow, on 29th January 1973. Watt was defending this title that night, as Buchanan had earlier relinquished it because of the Roberto Duran contest in

© Newsquest (Herald & Times)

Ken Buchanan and Jim Watt

1972. Buchanan won a hard contest on points. John Quinn, a boxing writer for the *Evening Times*, revealed a humorous story to newspaper colleague Alan Davidson concerning the aftermath of the contest that evening. John Quinn was in a lift with Buchanan and several others on their way back to Buchanan's dressing room. Quinn recalls the story to Davidson:

> There were about eight of us in that lift and it got stuck between the floors. Ken (Buchanan) was exhausted and dehydrated after a momentous fight. A couple of us managed to prise the doors open to circulate air and I'll always remember that just at that moment a colleague, who was also a pal, peered down at us through a crack in the doors. The late James 'Solly' Sanderson was quite an operator and he asked if I had any quotes from Ken. You can imagine my

> reply, but I must say I still chuckle about it when I
> look back.   (*Evening Times*, 3rd June, 2004)

Like Buchanan, Watt also would go on to glory as a professional, winning the vacant lightweight world title at the Kelvin Hall against Alfredo Pitalua in April 1979. Successful defences against Roberto Vasquez, Charlie Nash, Howard Davis and Sean O'Grady followed. The O'Grady contest was a particularly bloody one; and I can remember my father smiling joyously with a cigar in his mouth outside the Kelvin Hall after reporting from ringside, the fight taking place in the early hours of the morning of November 1st, 1980. His pearl-white shirt was heavily blood-spattered from the discharge from O'Grady's cut forehead, which had opened up to a torrent that streamed down the front of the boxer's face, resulting in the fight being stopped.

*

On the footballing front during the latter part of Sanderson's *Scottish Daily Express* career, Celtic had dominated the domestic game in Scotland from 1965 to 1974, winning the league title nine times in a row. In Europe, Celtic had won the European Cup in 1967, and had also defeated Leeds in 1970 in the semi-finals of the European Cup, only to lose to Feyenoord in the final that year (although earlier in the competition Celtic had ridden their luck going through on a toss of a coin against Benfica in the second round). Celtic very nearly reached the European Cup Final in 1972, but lost to Inter Milan in the semi-final at Parkhead after a penalty shoot-out, with Dixie Deans missing his spot-kick. Celtic again reached the semi-finals in 1974, losing to Athletico Madrid.

Rangers had been the first Scottish club to reach a European Final (the European Cup Winners' Cup) in 1961, but had lost to Fiorentina over two legs 4-1 on aggregate. They had again reached the European Cup Winners' Cup Final in 1967, but lost to Bayern Munich 1-0 in Nuremberg. Rangers finally enjoyed success in the European Cup Winners' Cup in 1972 beating Moscow Dynamo 3-2 in Barcelona (although unfortunately Rangers supporters clashed with Spanish police leading to a European ban).

The pedigree in Europe of both the Glasgow clubs was strong. Often Sanderson would travel behind the 'Iron Curtain' and visit countries such as Russia, East Germany or Czechoslovakia to cover European ties. Speaking of the Czech army side Dukla Prague of past years, Sanderson observed:

> In the old days, they operated a strange team selection process – if you were good, you became a Colonel. If you weren't, you peeled the potatoes.
> (Scottish Television interview, 1986)

Fortunes were improving for the national game, as in 1973, the Scottish national football team had qualified for the World Cup Finals in Munich '74. Added spice was given in that England had not made it. The Scottish team had been good, but scored too few goals. They had drawn 0-0 with Brazil (with Billy Bremner coming agonisingly close to scoring), and 1-1 with Yugoslavia, but in their first match had only managed to beat Zaire by 2-0, and failed to qualify for the next stage on goal difference. Sanderson was disgusted with the treatment manager Willie Ormond received in the aftermath of the campaign.

Also in 1974, Sanderson was handed his strangest

assignment by the *Express*. He had been reporting on the Commonwealth Games in New Zealand, and was ordered to make his way to Australia by his employers. His brief had nothing to do with sport, he was to meet up with the wife of Ronnie Biggs and see if he could persuade her to give her story to the *Express*. The *Express* editor, Ian MacColl, wanted Sanderson to visit Melbourne and make contact with Charmaine Biggs. The idea was to run an exclusive scoop on how she and train robber Ronnie Biggs had managed to evade capture for such a length of time after the 'Great Train Robbery'. The world authorities had tried desperately to find them and bring Biggs to justice – he was living a natural family life in Australia instead of being behind bars serving his prison sentence in the UK.

Sanderson befriended the Biggs' Australian neighbours and asked to take them to dinner (on *Express* expenses); he also cheekily got them to invite Charmaine Biggs by phone, and she had agreed. All was going to plan as they sat in a restaurant awaiting the appearance of Mrs Biggs that evening, but she never showed. A chance phone call she had made to her neighbours an hour before the meeting to check the arrangement had led to a discussion as to who the mystery guest from Scotland was. On hearing a story of a journalist who had made his way from the Commonwealth Games in Christchurch, New Zealand, Mrs Biggs had become suspicious as to the motive for the invite. She remained uncontactable and Sanderson never met her. The *Express* realised their mission was compromised, and Sanderson was recalled home. Charmaine Bigg's reluctance to meet up with unknown persons that evening was indeed well justified, as it would later transpire that plots to kidnap Ronnie Biggs by mercenaries were aplenty.

In the same year, the *Scottish Daily Express* headquarters at Albion Street in Glasgow were closed; which resulted in mass redundancies as operations were switched to a Manchester base. Sanderson, like many others at the time, had no choice but to take redundancy, and then see where his future career would lie. Mirror Group Newspapers offered Sanderson and his colleague Jim Rodger positions on the *Scottish Daily Mirror*, based at Anderston Quay, Glasgow. It would be during this spell in his newspaper career that Sanderson would cover the 1978 World Cup Finals in Argentina.

Chapter 2: Argentina 1978 –
The Flower of Scotland Wilts

We're on the march with Ally's Army,
we're going to the Argentine.
And we'll really shake them up,
when we win the World Cup,
'cos Scotland are the greatest football team.

> World Cup 1978 song (chorus),
> sung by Andy Cameron

The euphoria and dangerous optimism that followed the qualification for the World Cup Finals in Argentina ended in a humiliation that pervaded the nation's psyche for years afterwards. There was some foundation for this optimism, in that by 1977 Scotland had a good football team. The problem would be that the World Cup Finals would be held a year too late for Scotland.

Jim Watt, who won the world lightweight championship against Alfredo Pitalua in Glasgow in April 1979, commented on the insufferable pressure that he felt under before the championship contest, partly because Scotland was desperate for sporting success following the failure in Argentina a year earlier.

Watt explained:

> Suddenly I felt as if I was having my head put in a
> noose as happened with Scotland manager Ally
> MacLeod. Scotland's sad exit from the World Cup in
> Argentina was still fresh and heavy in the minds of all
> Scots. Ally had not been forgiven for the broken
> promises and now I sensed that everybody was
> looking at me to put some pride back into our sport.
>
> (*Watt's My Name*, 1981, page 68)

The 'broken promises' referred to was MacLeod's
confident prediction that Scotland would return from
Argentina with a medal at least. Scotland had qualified
from a small group of three, the other teams being Wales
and Czechoslovakia. Scotland had beaten Wales 1-0 at
Hampden in November 1976, having lost a month earlier
in Prague to the Czechs 2-0. Scotland had then beaten the
Czechs 3-1 at home in September 1977, then Wales 2-0 (at
Anfield, Liverpool) the following month.

Optimism had risen in Scotland due to what was seen
as a favourable group draw for the Finals. Peru, Iran and
Holland had been drawn in Scotland's group, and hopes
were high that Scotland could progress to the latter stages
of the tournament by securing at least second place in the
group. There were only four groups comprising four teams
– a total of 16 finalists. The SFA had arranged a send-off
for the squad from Hampden Park, as the players were
paraded in front of a well-wishing public of around 30,000
on an open-topped bus. The scenes would be in stark
contrast to the 22-man squad's return.

Prior to leaving for Argentina the players had been in
the glare of publicity. There was the dubious advertising

deal where the Scotland team promoted car sales by bizarrely heading footballs (in a Scotland strip) while sitting in a Chrysler car with the window down. Alan Rough, the Scotland keeper at the time, acquiesced toward current hair style fashion of the time by getting a perm (along with several others) and had appeared on the children's programme *Blue Peter* shortly before leaving for Argentina. They had presented him with a pennant displaying the *Blue Peter* ship logo for good luck. Rough had told the viewers that he would put the pennant behind his goal during the matches in Argentina. Unfortunately there would be plenty of opportunity to see it!

The squad was followed to South America by the usual gaggle of seasoned sports journalists, including James Sanderson who was now writing for the *Scottish Daily Mirror.* On this World Cup expedition Sanderson would use his guile and experience to ensure that he would land the top stories from the campaign. His years of experience working abroad meant he had learned the tricks of the journalistic trade, including 'bunging' (paying) individuals who had contacts that could help get information. The drama that unfolded in Argentina was perfect for a journalist with the ability to get the information for a scoop.

The first game in Cordoba against Peru took place on Saturday, 3rd June. However, Sanderson had realised that Ally MacLeod's squad was facing serious problems. Prior to Argentina the Home International Championships had taken place, where Scotland annually played Northern Ireland, Wales and England. The Scottish side had looked poor, particularly against Wales at Hampden, where key defender Gordon McQueen had badly injured his leg. Also at that game was the manager of Iran, Heshmat

Mohajerani, who noted weaknesses in the Scotland team. Later in Argentina he told Sanderson:

> If Scotland play as they did against Wales then there is every chance they won't qualify in our section. They have great players but I went to the game against Wales without telling anyone – and Scotland were bad. I saw a lot of flaws, and it has made my players confident. We could cause a major upset.
>
> (*Scottish Daily Mirror*, May 30th, 1978)

The warm-up games via the Home International championship had resulted in draws with Northern Ireland and Wales (both 1-1), and defeat to England 1-0. All the games had been played at Hampden Park. Sanderson had been critical of MacLeod's decision not to take Andy Gray (then of Aston Villa) to Argentina, feeling that Gray would give Scotland more firepower in South America.

After the 3-1 defeat to Peru it was the name of Cubillas, with his spectacular free kicks that had left keeper Alan Rough motionless as the net had bulged behind him, that was being uttered by a shocked nation back home in Scotland. Scotland had started well, had taken the lead through Joe Jordan, and had then been awarded a penalty. Then things nose-dived. A Scottish penalty miss by Don Masson was followed by three goals from the ageing Peruvian team. In the after-match post mortem that in fact lasted a few days, Sanderson wrote of MacLeod:

> He faces strong criticism for fielding the wrong team and adopting the wrong tactics. And the feeling of Scots supporters here was summed up by one small, sad-faced fan who said, "If you see MacLeod ask him when Jock Stein is becoming manager."
>
> (*Scottish Daily Mirror*, June 5th, 1978)

In the same article, Sanderson went on to say:

> He (MacLeod) is being attacked for selecting out-of-
> form players and accused of underestimating the
> danger from the Peruvian team.

MacLeod had been facing accusations by the press that
he had not done his homework on the Peruvian opposition,
and did not help his cause by stating to Sanderson:

> We did do our homework. Although I did not travel
> to see them, I went over TV clips again and again.

Worse was to follow. Sanderson was contacted by an
Argentinean journalist, whom he had befriended at the
Argentina v Scotland game in Buenos Aires in June 1977, a
year earlier. Had he heard the rumour that a Scotland
player had failed a routine drugs test? Sanderson was
asked.

Thus the story was broken under the headline: 'MY
SHAME! I Took Drugs Says Banned Soccer Star'. Willie
Johnston of West Bromwich Albion had taken two stimulant
pills (Reativa) just before the Peru game, then had taken
part in a random drugs test along with Kenny Dalglish
after the game, and had been found to have used illegal
substances that were banned by FIFA. Johnston was sent
home immediately in disgrace, although his actions were
largely due to ignorance. He had not realised that the pills
prescribed for him by his doctor at home would have the
potential repercussions by falling foul of the dope test.

As an experienced journalist, Sanderson did his
homework and interviewed Dr Gottfried Schoenhaltzer, the
Swiss chairman of FIFA's anti-doping control committee.
The drug discovered in Johnston's urine was identified as

Fencamfamin, a ". . . stimulant for fatigue and depression" (*Scottish Daily Mirror*, June 6th, 1978). It was not normally used to control hay fever which Johnston suffered from.

The SFA was worried in case Scotland would be thrown out of the tournament, and the FIFA executive committee considered meeting to discuss events. By immediately sending Johnston home the Scots camp was informed that they had acted appropriately in the circumstances.

The next game for Scotland was against Iran in Cordoba, and they would have to record a big win to give them any realistic hope of qualification to the next stage. Scotland played poorly, and drew 1-1, the Scots goal coming courtesy of an Iranian own goal. Fans that had travelled over to Argentina were now turning on the team, and the team bus was stoned. Sanderson reported events after the draw:

> They hurled stones and spat at the players' coach (bus) after Scotland scraped a lucky 1-1 draw against Iran. The fans screamed and shouted at the players when they climbed into the coach at Cordoba Stadium, Argentina. But the worst abuse was reserved for team manager Ally MacLeod who left the dressing rooms last. One burly blond fan shouted: "We've walked a million miles for f___ all."
>
> (*Scottish Daily Mirror,* June 8th, 1978)

In fact the Iranian manager had strongly fancied his team's chances against Scotland, sensing that the squad was in disarray. He told Sanderson before the game that he did not see Scotland scoring any goals against Iran, a statement that had an element of truth considering an Iranian player scored the Scots goal.

Ernst Happel, the Dutch manager, was noting events. Happel had been manager of Feyenoord when they defeated Jock Stein's Celtic in the 1970 European Cup Final at the San Siro, Milan. Happel was Austrian, and had earned 51 caps playing for the Austrian national team. Later he would again win the European Cup in 1983, managing a Hamburg side that would defeat Juventus 1-0 in Athens.

The Dutch team had expected themselves and Scotland to qualify for the last eight places. The Dutch had beaten Iran 3-0, and Happel had told Sanderson,

> "It is strange to me that so many of your players have lost their form."
>
> *(Scottish Daily Mirror,* June 10th,1978)

There existed a glimmer of hope because of the result between Holland and Peru. They had drawn 0-0. Scotland now had only one point from two games, and would have to beat the Dutch (who now had three points) by three clear goals in their final game to advance to the next stage. This was a task that appeared extremely unlikely. The game would take place in Mendoza. Meanwhile Peru (also on three points) were favourites to beat Iran in their last group match, and duly did so 4-1, coming top of the group with five points.

The Scottish sojourn had experienced a range of problems in Argentina. Training had been disrupted, the facilities and accommodation had been poor, there had been injuries to the squad, and mosquito bites had also added to the malaise. The game against Holland on 11th June 1978 was the last chance of Scotland salvaging some pride.

On reflection, there is nothing more Scottish than a wee man defiantly waving his fist having succeeded against insurmountable odds. This is of course the Archie Gemmill wonder-goal, immortalised in the film *Trainspotting*, and showcased at the Scottish Football Museum at Hampden Park. A moment of genius that for years has been a sweetener to counteract at least some of the bitter taste of failure in Argentina.

The glorious failure against the Dutch started with Scotland going behind 1-0, getting tantalisingly close at 3-1 (requiring one more goal to qualify), before Johnny Rep's thunderbolt pegged back Scotland to 3-2. Ernst Happel, the Holland manager, had confided in Sanderson two days before the match that the Dutch would be happy to taste defeat by the odd goal so long as they went through as runners-up in the group. This was a tactical decision, to avoid winning Group 4 and so avoid Argentina and Brazil in the second round. In the second round the Dutch met Italy, West Germany and Austria, all European teams. They avoided Argentina, Brazil and Poland, who played Peru instead.

Sanderson reported the discussion with the title: 'We could be better off losing – Happel.' The story read:

> Holland are so sure Scotland cannot pip them for a last-eight World Cup place that they are even prepared to LOSE tomorrow's clash by the odd goal to avoid finishing as winners of Group Four!

> Coach Ernst Happel outlined his thinking yesterday when he said that the Dutch would like to avoid Brazil in the second groupings, despite the poor form shown so far by the South American pre-tournament favourites.

The report went on later to quote Happel saying:

> It does not matter if we lose narrowly to Scotland.
> Peru will beat Iran and if the Peruvians then finish
> top of the group that could suit us. We do not want to
> meet Brazil if that can be avoided. And if we finish
> second then it looks as if we shall avoid them as it
> seems the best they can manage in their group is also
> second place.

Sanderson also revealed in the same article that Happel
had been happy to alter his squad for the Scotland game.

> Happel's announcement that he will make changes
> for the match with the Scots in Mendoza underlines
> his belief that the MacLeod 'miracle' is not on.
> (*Scottish Daily Mirror,* June 10th, 1978)

Whether this was merely bluster from Happel is
conjecture. For the record, the Dutch won the Second
Round Group A, meeting the hosts Argentina in the Final
(winners of Second Round Group B). Argentina won the
World Cup, as Sanderson had predicted prior to the start
of the competition finals, with a score of 3-1 after extra
time.

After the glorious failure of the Holland match, it was
clear that MacLeod had no intention of resigning, despite
mounting criticism and pressure. Sanderson was calling for
his resignation, touting Jock Stein as the ideal replacement.
Sanderson had written:

> Happel at first so feared Scotland that he has had
> their every move watched. But the dossier now before
> him simply damns the tartan army (the team) as the
> least prepared team in the World Cup.
> (*Scottish Daily Mirror,* June 10th, 1978)

Ally MacLeod announces his squad for Argentina.
Sanderson (in the pin-striped suit) casts an eye over
the squad selection

Sanderson was critical of the lack of preparation by MacLeod, the poor training facilities and some of the judgments that had been made. Against Peru, Sanderson had advocated that Scotland bombard the small Peruvian defenders with high balls, in order that the big men up front could make good use of their physical advantage. He was irritated that Andy Gray was left home in Britain; that Graeme Souness had only been used in the final match in Mendoza; and that Derek Johnstone had never been played in any of the matches, even though he had scored both goals in the Home International Championships, one against Northern Ireland and one against Wales. Johnstone had then been rewarded for his efforts by being dropped by MacLeod for the final game against England. Derek Johnstone had made the 40 goals mark scored that season.

Sanderson campaigned for Stein to be immediately appointed as the replacement Scotland manager, but MacLeod was not going to go easily. MacLeod had said to journalists after the win over Holland:

> There may be an execution squad waiting for me, but deep down I still admire myself.
>
> (*Scottish Daily Mirror*, 12th June, 1978)

Scotland had given one of their finest performances against the Dutch, and opinion was divided as to whether this was enough to save MacLeod's job. Sanderson's opinions voiced on a Radio Clyde Sunday phone-in shortly after the Scotland team returned led to heated debate. It would be the start of an eight-year association with Radio Clyde football phone-ins.

The Scottish domestic game was soon to enter a new era, one that would be dominated by the success of the 'New Firm'.

James Sanderson meets Rhodesian Prime Minister Ian Smith in 1970. Their views on the need for a white heavyweight champion did not concur, as seems evident from Sanderson's expression

Chapter 3: The Emergence of the New Firm

The dominance of Scottish football by Celtic and Rangers was to be challenged from 1979 to 1985 by what was termed the New Firm from the north east of Scotland, namely Aberdeen and Dundee United. This had serious implications for both Celtic and Rangers, and their supporters, in that their teams' long dominance in Scotland was checked.

Indicative of the desperation felt at the time were the disgraceful scenes at Hampden Park at the end of an Old Firm Scottish Cup Final in May 1980. Certainly alcohol was the main contributor to events of battling rival supporters who charged onto the pitch after Celtic had narrowly won a tense match 1-0 in extra time. It also marked the fact that both Celtic and Rangers were anxious to win some silverware that year, with Aberdeen having wrapped up the Premier League that season, and Dundee United having won the League Cup.

Unfortunately, on that hot day, an American marching band had been invited to play prior to the match. What they must have thought as the scene of violence unfolded at the final whistle God only knows, but the shameful scenes were broadcast worldwide, a sad reminder of the hatred and division that perpetuates from generation to generation of hopefully now only a small minority of Old Firm supporters.

As well as the old sectarian problem, Scottish football would also be met with economic problems. Margaret Thatcher's Conservative government having been elected in 1979, the following severe recession would cause unemployment to spiral particularly in Scotland, with its reliance on industries such as heavy engineering and manufacturing. This would have a dramatic effect on football attendances. The game would effectively go into the doldrums in terms of gate receipts.

For Rangers in particular, this would be a barren time. In the season of 1974/75 Rangers had managed to halt Celtic's dominance curtailing the nine-in-a-row sequence that Celtic had accumulated from 1965 to 1974. The league title had then exchanged hands between the Old Firm, with Rangers winning the league championship in 1975/76 and 1977/78; and Celtic in 1976/77 and 1978/79. The old format of two divisions with 18 teams was changed to introduce a Premier League and Divisions One and Two from 1975. Rangers would have to wait a period of nine seasons before once again tasting league championship success in the 1986/87 season. It would not be the best of times for the Ibrox faithful.

By 1980 the mould had been finally broken by one half of the 'New Firm', with Aberdeen finally interrupting years of Old Firm supremacy by capturing the league title in season 1979/80. Not since the 1964/65 season had there been a team outside of the Old Firm that had experienced this success, with Kilmarnock having been the victors in 1965. Times were changing in Scottish football, and a significant threat to the power of the Old Firm was emerging. Aberdeen, led by Alex Ferguson, (and ably assisted by Archie Knox for a time until he took the managerial job at Dundee) and Dundee United with Jim McLean as manager, were about to give the Old Firm a run for their money over the next five years or so.

*

In the sport of boxing, Jim Watt would lose his world lightweight title on points to Nicaraguan-born Alexis Arguello in the Wembley Arena, London, in 1981 in the fifth defence of his title. Watt would not fight again, but would be worshipped by the Scottish boxing fraternity, delighted to have seen success at World Championship level.

Shortly before the Arguello fight Jimmy Sanderson had been asked his opinion of the likely outcome on both radio and television. Sanderson replied, "My heart says Watt, but my head says Arguello, and I can't let my heart rule my head." In the same interview, Sanderson had been asked his opinion on the existence of boxing cartels in the sport. He replied: "There have been cartels in the sport of boxing since Cain and Abel, and that was not a particularly good fight!"

At this point in time, the Radio Clyde station operated from fairly small premises situated above the shopping centre and bus station at Anderston Cross, Glasgow. In the mid-1980s they would move to new premises in Clydebank following ten years of success since their inception. Their logo was 'Radio Clyde 261', indicating the radio frequency they could be found on at the time. As a commercial radio station, dependent on advertising revenue, it was important that a strong sports section was in place to woo listeners, and thus generate much needed income. Their rivals at BBC Radio Scotland could rely on funding from licence-fee collection.

An advantage that Radio Clyde had was to be able to focus the majority of attention towards the fortunes of the Old Firm, being a local station for the west of Scotland. As the Old Firm historically carried by far the greatest support in Scotland in terms of fans attending the matches and armchair supporters at home, this was important for listening figures. Another important factor was that it was common practice for supporters in the west of Scotland to tune into the phone-in as they departed the grounds by car to hear scores and match reports from other games. Thus a strong sports programme was essential for this strategy, and Sanderson would play an important part in this success. It was Sanderson who advocated that supporters at matches should always 'Take their tranny (transistor radio)' to listen in on the fortunes of their rivals at another game while watching their beloved team.

Alan Davidson of the *Evening Times* sums up the success of the Radio Clyde phone-in from its early days, looking back over some twenty years ago:

> The radio phone-in was an excellent and hugely humorous concept when it was introduced in the '80s by West of Scotland broadcaster Radio Clyde, utilising the acerbic talents of the late James Sanderson. The man known in the trade as 'Solly' was an original

innovator on the airwaves, winding up and badgering his audiences with his clipped tones and dismissive replies.

(Evening Times, 17th May, 2005)

Over time the listening audience would be exposed to familiar words and phrases on the programme such as 'bunkum!'; 'balderdash!'; 'I don't change horses in mid-stream'; 'I don't give tips, just opinions'; 'I don't tell football managers how to do their job, and they don't tell me how to do mine'; 'I don't sit on the fence' and of course, 'Are you accusing me of mendacity?' which seemed to pass into football phone-in folklore as some poor punter on the receiving end wondered what the hell he was talking about.

However, it would be the accusatory confrontation of 'Were you at the game?' that would become Sanderson's signature phrase, as he grilled phone-in callers live on the air to account for their particular whereabouts when that day's matches had commenced.

A good Celtic team managed by Billy McNeill would be victorious in winning two keenly fought league campaigns in 1980/81 and again in 1981/82. Celtic's team was fairly strong at that point in time, with players including Pat Bonner, Danny McGrain, Roy Aitken, Tommy Burns, Davie Provan and Murdo MacLeod in their ranks. Celtic had also unearthed a talented young goal-scorer called Charlie Nicholas, who Sanderson would name 'the Cannonball Kid'. Nicholas would leave Celtic to join Arsenal in the summer of 1983, a move Sanderson criticised as he felt that Nicholas had joined the wrong club. Sanderson had felt that Liverpool would be the correct choice for Nicholas, and he knew that the Liverpool captain, Graeme Souness, had tried to persuade Nicholas to join him at Anfield. On a

Scotland tour of Canada in June 1983, Sanderson reported:

> Charlie Nicholas, the Cannonball Kid, has dropped a clanger – by joining the wrong club. So says Scotland manager Jock Stein, who believes: 'Liverpool were the right club for Charlie – for footballing reasons'.
>
> (*Scottish Daily Mirror*, June 11th, 1983)

Sanderson had believed that the style of play at Arsenal would not suit Nicholas, and he thought that Nicholas teaming up with Kenny Dalglish and Ian Rush at Liverpool as a strike force was a far more suitable option.

At Ibrox, Rangers, with John Greig as manager, struggled. They would have to rely on domestic cup competitions to deliver any success for their supporters. They would attempt to appease their fans with a Scottish Cup victory in 1981 as they defeated Dundee United 4-1 after a replay, and a League cup win in the 1981/82 season again against Dundee United, the score being 2-1. At this point in time, the key players for Rangers were Davie Cooper, John McClelland, Jim Bett, Ally Dawson and team veterans Peter McCloy and Derek Johnstone. Sandy Jardine, another great servant for Rangers, moved to Hearts in 1982.

The Scotland team had qualified for the World Cup Finals for the third time in a row, but would attend the event in Spain in the month of June 1982 with some trepidation, the bad memories of the Argentina 1978 campaign still fresh in the minds of the nation. The Scots would again fail to progress to the later stages, and as was becoming a habit, only a total of three games played would be the summation of the Scots contribution to the tournament. Scotland started well, with a 5-2 victory against New Zealand in the opening game in Malaga. The rare feat of Scotland scoring a large number of goals was tarnished slightly by letting New Zealand back into the match. The Scots had been 3-0 up, but then had lost two goals, before scoring another two. This game was followed by a 4-1 defeat to Brazil in Seville after David Narey had annoyed the Brazilians by having the audacity to score first with a scorcher of a shot (or merely a toe-poke if you were Jimmy Hill).

The last game would be memorable for all the wrong reasons. In a 2-2 draw with the USSR back in Malaga, a game that Scotland required to win, Joe Jordan gave Scotland hope by opening the scoring. Later in the game, the Scots nation would look on in horror as defenders Alan Hansen and Willie Miller were involved in a mix-up and collided with one another, leading to a goal for the USSR. Again, Scotland would exit a World Cup Finals after the first round on goal difference.

The well-worn excuse that Scotland was too small a nation to expect to be good enough to progress past the preliminary stage of the World Cup Finals was on this occasion found to be moribund. "It doesn't seem to have deterred the Northern Irish," Sanderson had pronounced on radio. "Scotland have delusions of adequacy, never mind delusions of grandeur," he chided.

Scotland and Northern Ireland had been in the same World Cup qualification group, and had seen off Sweden, Portugal, and Israel. At the 1982 World Cup Finals the Northern Irish came top of their first round group (Group E), and had beaten hosts Spain 1-0 to boot. Thus the Northern Irish had done what Scotland to date never have, i.e. progressed past the first round of a World Cup Finals. England had also competed in Spain in 1982, having been in the World Cup wilderness since the 1970 Finals in Mexico.

Sanderson had correctly tipped Italy as the likely winners of the 1982 World Cup prior to attending the Finals in Spain, and the Italians obliged, beating West Germany 3-1 in the climax of the tournament. More teams played in the 1982 World Cup Finals, with a total of 24 qualifying, as opposed to only 16 for Argentina 1978.

Back in the Scottish domestic game, the New Firm was about to intensify its presence as a power in Scottish football. Dundee United would win the 1982/83 Premier League with a small squad, but with quality players such as Hamish McAlpine, Richard Gough, Paul Sturrock, Eamonn Bannon, Paul Hegarty, David Narey and Davie Dodds. They just edged out Aberdeen and Celtic in a very tight league run-in. Celtic's campaign was derailed as they suffered defeats to both Dundee United and Aberdeen in the closing stages of the title race. Aberdeen would achieve European glory that same season in the 1983 European Cup Winners' Cup. Sanderson wrote about these achievements in his *Scottish Daily Mirror* column:

> In the week in which Aberdeen won the European Cup Winners' Cup Dundee United are set to show that the game has swung away from the once arrogant West. It would be final recognition for the North East clubs, who have long suffered under the cruel insult of being just 'country cousins' to Rangers and Celtic.

In the same article he elaborated (speaking of Jim McLean and Alex Ferguson):

> . . . it shows that McLean and Alex Ferguson are the
> new forces and that Glasgow takes second place. That
> is no bad thing, despite what others might say.
>
> And, for the North East, after having had to take so
> many insults and so much stick down the years of
> Rangers and Celtic domination, it would be a richly
> rewarding time for the clubs deserving to be called
> the 'New Firm'.
>
> (*Scottish Daily Mirror*, May 14th, 1983)

This would not be all for Aberdeen, as future domestic
success would deliver the Premier title for 1983/84 and in
1984/85. Also in the Scottish Cup Aberdeen would be
victorious three times on the trot, winning it in 1982, 1983
and 1984. To underline their superiority to the Old Firm,
they confidently arrived at Hampden in the Old Firm's
back yard of Glasgow to beat Rangers in the 1982 Scottish
Cup Final 4-1 after extra time; defeat Rangers the
following year 1-0 after extra time to lift the 1983 Scottish
Cup; and beat Celtic 2-1 in the 1984 Scottish Cup final, yet
again in extra time.

Rangers and Celtic would seek solace in relying on the
League Cup for trophy success. Celtic would win it in 1983
beating Rangers 2-1, and Rangers would win it for the next
two seasons; defeating Celtic for the 1984 League cup 3-2
in extra time, and defeating Dundee United in the 1985
League cup final 1-0. These successes would not be enough
to placate the Old Firm support, as it was clear that the
better football from 1983 in Scotland was not emanating
from the Glasgow sides.

The success of Aberdeen in Europe in 1983 proved
particularly galling for Old Firm supporters, who for years

had considered these achievements as possible only for Scottish clubs with an historical large support, i.e. Celtic and Rangers. They looked on with envy and admiration as Alex Ferguson guided a talented Aberdeen squad to European glory. Aberdeen were narrowly beaten to the Premier title by Dundee United in the 1982/83 season, but all of Scotland marvelled at Aberdeen's European exploits culminating in success in Gothenburg beating Real Madrid 2-1 after extra-time on a rain-drenched pitch. Aberdeen had opened the scoring through Eric Black, but Real Madrid equalised via a penalty from Juanito. Eric Black was replaced with John Hewitt, and Hewitt grabbed victory for the Dons with a diving header from a superb cross from Mark McGhee. The travelling Aberdeen support in Europe that season was officially voted the best behaved by UEFA.

This was a particularly strong Aberdeen squad, which would guarantee dominance in Scotland for the following two years. They would also provide many of the key Scottish international players. Alex McLeish and Gordon Strachan (who would become future managers of Rangers and Celtic respectively); as well as Jim Leighton and Willie Miller, would all be stalwarts of the Scotland squad.

From the mid-1980s the Radio Clyde football phone-in would be adorned with a queue of Old Firm supporters ranting and raving with frustration, united in their opinion and in their fear of a common enemy from the northeast of Scotland. It was a difficult enough fixture to play away at both Pittodrie and Tannadice, but now Aberdeen and Dundee United were fearless when visiting the Old Firm on their own turf. Times had changed, and the Old Firm support did not like what they were seeing.

"I think that you are in a minority of one!" Sanderson

bellowed in reply to a Radio Clyde caller who dared to opine that the New Firm threat was merely an illusion.

Such was the perceived strength of Aberdeen at the time that Sanderson wrote prior to the season starting for 1983/84:

> Put your shirt on the Red Devils of Aberdeen to win the red-hot Premier Division as the season starts today. Alex Ferguson's men, European Cup Winners' Cup conquerors of Real Madrid in Gothenburg, have the talent, individually and collectively, to take the flag. No pussyfooting about that.
>
> (*Scottish Daily Mirror,* August 20th, 1983)

Aberdeen duly delivered.

Chapter 4: Crisis, What Crisis?

The Home International Championship, played annually with Wales, Northern Ireland and England was waning in popularity. Certainly the Scotland v England clash was always a sell-out, such was the defiance against the 'Auld Enemy' from the Scots. However the games against Northern Ireland and Wales were now fairly poorly attended, and there was little enthusiasm for the two fixtures which had diminished in popularity. It would soon be time to call a halt to the Home International Championship competition.

Sanderson had been asked to speak on STV about the debate regarding scrapping the tournament, and expressed the view that, "It has had its day. Anyone who misses the competition is crying crocodile tears." Bertie Auld, one of the legendary Lisbon Lions, had been invited to debate the case, and to put forward reasons why the competition should be retained.

Scotland were playing Northern Ireland at Hampden that night in May 1983, and Sanderson was driving to Hampden Park after the brief TV slot to report on it. Before the pair went on air, Auld mentioned to Sanderson that unfortunately he would not be able to attend the match that evening, as he had a prior engagement. Sanderson said nothing, until, that was, they were live on air. After Auld had put forward a nostalgic reason for preserving the competition, Sanderson leant over and said, "But Bertie, you aren't going to the match tonight!"

Auld looked like a rabbit caught in car headlights. Sanderson had gone for the kill. Around 16,000 souls turned up on a rainy evening at Hampden that night to witness a dull 0-0 draw.

*

Earlier in March 1983 Premier league attendances had drastically diminished in Scotland, and it was becoming clear that in Scottish football all was not well. At that time the Premier division consisted of 10 clubs in total. In the *Scottish Daily Mirror,* Sanderson wrote under the headline "The Sad Crisis Facing Scottish Soccer":

> Last Saturday's gates in the Premier Division plunged to a new low. But instead of recognising that fact, the clubs are engaged in political in-fighting that could result in the deaths of some. It is sad that Saturday's figures should be so shameful. They totalled a mere 29,625 – an average of 5,965.
>
> (*Scottish Daily Mirror,* March 9th, 1983)

In the same article, Sanderson also noted, "Rangers attendances have plunged this year." One main reason for this of course was the factor of the lack of success the club was experiencing at this time.

A sample of Premier League attendance figures for home games played at Ibrox in early 1983 illustrates this

The lowest crowd for an international at Hampden was the 7,455 who saw Scotland draw with N. Ireland in May 1969

point (Celtic is omitted as this fixture was always well attended).

Ibrox Attendances

v.	Date	Attendance
DUNDEE UTD	January 8th, 1983	15,500
KILMARNOCK	January 15th, 1983	11,223
DUNDEE	February 5th, 1983	8,500
HIBERNIAN	March 5th, 1983	10,975
MOTHERWELL	March 19th, 1983	18,000
ABERDEEN	April 9th, 1983	19,800
MORTON	April 23rd, 1983	9,500
ST MIRREN	April 30th, 1983	9,321

Source: *Rangers: The Complete Record* p558
Bob Ferrier and Robert McElroy (2005)

The exciting climax to the 1982/83 season helped to some extent to boost average attendances elsewhere as Dundee United, Aberdeen and Celtic competed for the Premier division title in a nail-biting finish.

David Ross in his book *The Roar of the Crowd* (2005) gives average attendance figures for Scottish clubs over the years, and this is extremely useful as a barometer to measure the general trends of supporters turning up for matches. In relation to the Old Firm he cites an average attendance per season at Ibrox and Parkhead. For the period 1978 to 1983 he gives the following statistics:

Average attendance for season (home matches)

Year	Celtic	Rangers
1978-79	25303	25628
1979-80	28499	20405
1980-81	22836	18328
1981-82	22718	16400
1982-83	23740	17681

Source: *The Roar of the Crowd* pps 101-102
David Ross (2005)

In season 1983/84 more difficulty was to follow for both Rangers and Celtic. John Greig was finally deposed as Rangers manager after a period of five testing years, having previously survived several rounds of votes of confidence from the Rangers board. After-match supporter demonstrations after disappointing results heaped more pressure on the four-man Rangers board, comprising of Chairman Rae Simpson, Vice-Chairman Jack Gillespie, with directors John Paton and Willie Waddell.

Greig went on 28th October, 1983. He had been only the sixth Rangers manager since World War II. One of his last signings would be Ally McCoist from Sunderland, which would in later years prove to be an inspired decision.

Sanderson had commented days before Greig's departure:

> But his five-year reign, with one-and-a-half million pounds spent, has been a failure. No-one can argue against that.
>
> (*Scottish Daily Mirror,* 24th October, 1983)

After Greig's departure it was Tommy McLean who had stepped into the breach as caretaker manager. Rangers suffered three defeats in a very bad week. Sanderson wrote on the matter:

> With three defeats – by St Mirren, Porto and Celtic – a boardroom power struggle, and the aftermath of the Greig resignation the club has been allowed to plummet to the depths in almost every sense. The £10 million pound ground sparkles in modernity, while a patchwork collection of a team staggers along with the air of men who have been left to struggle in a quagmire of indecision and mediocrity, without any leadership whatsoever.
>
> (*Scottish Daily Mirror,* November 7th, 1983)

A joke going around Glasgow pubs at the time concerned the fact that the newly built spectator stands at Ibrox were rumoured to have serious structural defects – they were facing the pitch. How things would be so different for Rangers five years or so into the future when the 'Ibrox revolution' would yield a dramatic transformation in the club's fortunes.

Although Alex Ferguson and Jim McLean were hotly tipped to take over the managerial reins at Ibrox, both declined the job, and it was Jock Wallace who eventually replaced Greig on November 10th, 1983. Wallace had previously managed Rangers prior to John Greig's stint before leaving to manage Leicester City in 1978. Wallace had then returned to Scotland to manage Motherwell, where David Hay had vacated the position. Having been appointed at Ibrox, Wallace then went on a short break to Spain and was roundly criticised for it. Sanderson, on the other hand, applauded this action as a positive step:

> I think it is the best thing he could do. He can sit
> quietly and sensibly take stock of the whole shambles
> that is Ibrox: A team in disarray and despair.
> (*Scottish Daily Mirror*, November 15th, 1983)

At Parkhead, Billy McNeill had left for Maine Road to manage Manchester City, and was replaced with David Hay in August 1983. Hay had been successful as manager of Motherwell, but had resigned to take up a job offer in the USA which had subsequently fallen through. He had been in the football wilderness for nearly a year.

There was dissent from the Celtic support with regard to the Celtic board. They had watched Celtic's playing staff become weakened with the sale of prize asset Charlie Nicholas to Arsenal, and George McCluskey to Leeds United, bringing in nearly one million pounds in transfer money. Celtic's firepower upfront had been seriously compromised, although they did have Frank McGarvey, and Billy McNeill had signed Brian McClair from Motherwell shortly before leaving the club for Manchester City. Celtic also had a new star player who was home-grown however, an eighteen year-old called Paul McStay.

There was frustration with the Celtic board from the Celtic fans, in that Celtic supporters were desperate to see that the money received from transfer sales would be immediately re-invested in top-class new signings to strengthen the squad, particularly in attack. An opportunity to sign a young player from Partick Thistle, Scotland Under-21 team member Maurice Johnston, was squandered by Celtic, and Johnston was signed by Watford instead for around £200,000.

Sanderson had voiced his concerns on Radio Clyde

over the matter, exclaiming that: "Celtic are like a Centurion tank without weapons." Celtic would later sign Maurice Johnston for £400,000 in October 1984 from Watford.

Dundee United competed in the European Cup, courtesy of being Premier League champions for 1982/83. They had a superb run, and reached the semi-final stages where they met Roma. Things looked promising for reaching the European Cup Final after a first leg 2-0 victory at Tannadice, however they were defeated 3-0 in the return leg at the Olympic stadium and crashed out of the competition. Roma lost in the Final to Liverpool in May '84.

Aberdeen also did well in Europe for season 1983/84, once again competing in the European Cup Winners' Cup, the trophy that they had won the year before. Like Dundee United, they also reached the semi-finals of a European competition that season, losing to Porto. The 'New Firm' had thus built their reputation as the Scottish clubs to fear in Europe, a mantle that had previously been owned by the 'Old Firm' in bygone years.

Fortunes had improved somewhat for Rangers with the return of Jock Wallace as manager, with a League Cup victory over Celtic. Celtic won nothing that '83/84 season, despite reaching two domestic Cup Finals, as they lost to Aberdeen in the Scottish Cup.

Aberdeen continued their dominance in Scotland, again winning the Premier title for 1984/85. Celtic won some silverware by defeating Dundee United in the Scottish Cup, and Rangers won the League Cup.

In Europe for '84/85 Scottish clubs did little of note. Aberdeen went out early in the European Cup to Dynamo Berlin, and Celtic lost to Rapid Vienna in the European Cup Winners' Cup in controversial circumstances after an ordered replay at Old Trafford (deemed a neutral venue) following a bottle-throwing incident at Parkhead. Rapid Vienna subsequently got to the final, and lost to Everton. In the UEFA Cup, Hearts went out to Paris St Germain, Rangers lost to Inter Milan, and Dundee United lost to Manchester United.

At international level, the British (Home International) Championship had at last been scrapped, the last fixtures being held in 1984. Later that year, Maurice (Mo) Johnston excelled as Scotland defeated Spain 3-1 at Hampden Park in a World Cup qualifier in November 1984. Scotland would have a see-saw experience in their attempt to qualify for Mexico 1986. Along with Scotland, the qualifying group consisted of Spain, Wales and Iceland. Scotland lost the home fixture to Wales in early 1985 1-0, a month after losing to Spain in Seville by the same score.

On Radio Clyde, who covered the game live that evening, Richard Park conducted a post-mortem of the match with Sanderson and guest broadcaster Ian St John. They were joined on the telephone by singer Rod Stewart, who was unable to attend the match at Hampden in person.

Richard Park: "And listening to the match in Los Angeles, in California, was one of Scotland's greatest supporters, Rod Stewart. I think Rod's on the line just now. Hello Rod?"

Rod Stewart: "Yes, hello, I'm here."

Richard Park: "Disappointing night for us!"

Rod Stewart: "Yes, just when I thought we had a team with a bit of consistency it seems that we've got to go back to the drawing board."

Richard Park: "Yes, this was one very disappointing night. James Sanderson is here again to have a very brief word with you, as he was of course in Seville a month ago when we also went down 1-0."

James Sanderson: "Well I hoped to bring you better news Rod, I'm sorry about that. But really, if you'd been here at Hampden you'd have seen something of a shambles of a Scotland team. As you say, it's back to the drawing board, but I don't know what kind of pictures we're going to start drawing. But perhaps Ian St John, whom you know, will be able to give you some better news than I can."

Ian St John: "Hi Rod."

Rod Stewart: "Hi there Ian, how are you?"

Ian St John: "Alright sir."

Rod Stewart: "It sounded dreadful on the radio".

Ian St John: "Honestly, I mean, this is the thing when you're talking to a radio audience, you don't want to paint a picture that's not true. We wanted Scotland to do so well tonight, and we were hoping that things were going to turn out. But the game just got worse and worse and worse, and it looked at the end of the game like a park's team."

This campaign for qualification for the World Cup Finals in Mexico 1986 would ultimately be remembered for one thing, the loss of the great Jock Stein.

© Newsquest (Herald & Times)

Jock Stein

Chapter 5: Tribute to Jock Stein

So much has been said about that fateful night in Cardiff when Scotland manager Jock Stein died of a heart attack as the game reached its closing stages. Perhaps one of Sanderson's most eloquent speeches on Radio Clyde was the day after Jock Stein died. Stein had collapsed at the end of the Wales v Scotland World Cup qualifier for Mexico 1986, held at Ninian Park on September 10th, 1985.

The game had finished 1-1, and Scotland still had a chance to qualify for the World Cup Finals. Scotland's equalising goal came from the penalty spot in the last ten minutes of the match, and was scored by the talented Davie Cooper. Some ten years later, Scotland would mourn the passing of Cooper as they had Stein.

The day after Jock Stein's death, Sanderson, live on Radio Clyde, gave a fitting epitaph to Stein, a man he had personally known for years. It was arguably Sanderson's best contribution to Scottish football on the radio – short, precise and moving. His tribute was as follows:

> Jock Stein believed that life should be as challenging and as rounded as the ball that dominated every one of his waking moments.

I did know him for thirty years and I have written today, and I can only repeat, I felt both the lash of his tongue and the warmth of his handshake.

I called him John and not Jock. I travelled the world with him, and really he is a man who taught me a great deal, and he is a man that I shall never forget.

And you've got to remember, that he did stride through football like a giant; revolutionising, revitalising, and casting a giant shadow.

I really think he enriched the game, and he most certainly enriched all of us who knew him.

Sanderson holds court at a black-tie event. Far left is the great Jock Stein seated beside Dougie Donnelly

Chapter 6: Crossing Swords

James Sanderson's career had been going well since events in Argentina 1978. The Radio Clyde phone-in was proving extremely popular with a large and loyal listening audience. He was also doing regular television appearances with Jim White on STV, providing opinion on the main events that were unfolding in Scottish football.

However, trouble was lurking around the corner for Sanderson, as from the summer of 1984 an event occurred that would have a significant impact on his life as a Scottish football writer. His main employer was the *Scottish Daily Mirror*, owned by Mirror Group Newspapers (MGN). In mid-1984 MGN was acquired by Robert Maxwell. A chill wind blew around Anderston Quay, Glasgow. Robert Maxwell had taken charge of the *Daily Record, Sunday Mail, Daily Mirror* and *Sunday People*.

Maxwell had the reputation of a bully, and it was anticipated that he would personally interfere with the editorial standards of MGN. These fears were not unfounded, and Maxwell's managerial style soon began to have a marked impact on the employees of the newspapers he now owned.

Maxwell's reputation gained through earlier forays in the newspaper industry in Scotland in the mid 1970s provided his newly acquired staff in 1984 with a good reason to be alarmed. Derek Bateman and Derek Douglas in their book *Unfriendly Games – Boycotted and Broke* (1986) discuss Maxwell's involvement in the ill-fated Commonwealth Games in Edinburgh in 1986. They also give an account of Maxwell's rise through his business dealings. One of the notable events was Maxwell's involvement with the short-lived newspaper, the *Scottish Daily News*.

Bateman and Douglas (p45–46) wrote:

> This was a workers' cooperative venture begun by those made redundant by the *Scottish Daily Express* as it closed its Albion Street headquarters in Glasgow in favour of a retreat to Manchester. They had sunk their severance cash into the project and Maxwell brought to the venture his business acumen, the Socialist credentials of a former Labour MP, and over £100,000 in cash, which represented £1 for every 50p the workforce had put in. From the outset it became apparent that the *Daily News* project might be a workers' cooperative but some of the workers were more equal than others. And the most equal of all was Robert Maxwell. He became the dominant personality, with the original chairman being ousted and a professional general manager being recruited from outside also being shown the door.
>
> The Maxwell tannoy announcements to the 500 staff with daily encouragement to work harder and meet the deadlines have passed into newspaper folklore

but it was all true. Eventually the project foundered. It probably never stood much of a chance anyway but along the way Maxwell reaped yet more unfavourable publicity with claims that he had hijacked what had been intended as a noble experiment by 500 newspaper workers determined to stay in the business and secure their livelihoods.

Indeed Maxwell's reign at MGN in the mid-1980s was to have catastrophic consequences for Sanderson. Maxwell had stamped his authority on the finances of MGN, where he utilised techniques gained in dealings earlier in his business career. He looked to ways of cost cutting, and one of his methods was to restrict the number of journalists he would send to cover sporting events. As MGN owned several newspaper titles, Maxwell did not want the expense of sending several journalists from his stable of newspapers to cover the same event. Maxwell decreed that he would restrict the number of journalists to be sent abroad for major sporting events, and Sanderson was told that Mirror Group Newspapers would not foot the bill for sending him to cover matches outside of Scotland for the *Scottish Daily Mirror.*

This was a slap in the face for Sanderson, as the Radio Clyde phone-in had generated extra sales for the *Scottish Daily Mirror* on the back of Sanderson's popularity. Richard Park would play the song 'Here Comes the Mirror Man' by the Human League to introduce Sanderson's radio slot. Sanderson's credibility as a top sports journalist was being compromised by the fact that his employing newspaper was refusing to send him to European and international football matches. Ironically his catchphrase, 'Were you at the game?' would now start to haunt him.

It was clear that things would come to a head, and Sanderson was boiling over with frustration. However, any employment lawyer will tell you that, as a general rule, an employer may not necessarily have a duty to provide work for an employee, as long as remuneration is given. On the other hand an employee has a duty to obey all lawful orders given by the employer (i.e. demonstrate obedience), and also has a duty of loyalty to the employer. These factors would become critical as events unfolded.

The first major problem for Sanderson was when Celtic had been ordered to replay a European Cup Winners' Cup tie against Rapid Vienna at Old Trafford in Manchester in mid-December 1984 (UEFA deeming this a neutral venue), as a result of a bottle-throwing incident at Parkhead at the November match in Glasgow where Celtic had 'gone through' on aggregate scores. Mirror Group Newspapers refused to sanction his trip, saying that his presence at the match was surplus to requirements for MGN.

Sanderson therefore arranged his own travel, and paid out of his own pocket to stay overnight in a Manchester hotel. Frank McGhee, the chief football writer for MGN in England was sent to cover the game instead, despite having no in-depth knowledge of Scottish football. Matters were to worsen quickly, as Scotland had to play Spain in Seville in late February 1985 as part of an important qualifier for the World Cup finals to be held in Mexico in 1986. Again Sanderson was refused by his employer to be sent to the fixture. Help was at hand from Radio Clyde, who arranged for Sanderson to go to Seville along with Richard Park and Paul Cooney. By this point Sanderson was livid at his treatment by Mirror Group Newspapers as his employer, and it was only a matter of time that his outspoken disposition would lead to severe consequences.

This manifested itself in an article in the 'Mr Glasgow' feature of Glasgow's *Evening Times* on February 22nd, 1985, less than a week before the Seville match. The *Evening Times* had heard rumours on the grapevine of Sanderson's plight and had called him to enquire as to what was happening at Mirror Group Newspapers over at Anderston Quay. In the resulting published article, Sanderson was as usual forthright, and also critical of his employer, Robert Maxwell. The article was headed 'Solly Goes Solo! – World Cup Shock For Sportswriter James'. It read:

> James 'Solly' Sanderson, who is proud to tell people that he has travelled the world reporting the deeds of the Scotland football team, told me a sorry tale today. He is travelling to Seville next week but he is having to pay his own way. That has never happened to the dapper Mr Sanderson before. Mr Sanderson was unequivocal in the reason for this state of affairs.
>
> "Captain Bob," he said, referring to his employer at the Daily Mirror, Mr Robert Maxwell, "obviously doesn't think that Scotland matters as far as the *Daily Mirror* is concerned."
>
> "Captain Bob doesn't seem to have any finance. I was told by the Manchester office that they couldn't afford to send either myself or Alan Nixon of the *Sunday Mirror*. It's a very sorry state of affairs."
>
> Mr Sanderson will be working for Radio Clyde while he's in Spain for the World Cup game on Wednesday, but Radio Clyde is not paying his fares either. Mr Sanderson, who is small but perfectly formed, had

just come off air at Radio Clyde with the latest news about football in his usual forthright and unmistakeable style.

He said: "I shall be working Monday, Tuesday and Wednesday and I'll be paid by the station for the work I do on air. You can say that I'll recoup my expenses through Radio Clyde and in other directions. Most certainly I will not be working for the *Daily Mirror*. I don't know what they'll do for coverage of the game, that's not my concern. They couldn't pay my expenses even though I'm chief sports writer."

It was with some regret that Mr Sanderson reminisced about the past. He said, "I've covered every World Cup since 1958 and now it's come to this. In fact, I think I'm the only one left who's been at World Cups since 1958 since Hugh Taylor retired. Concerned about what I've said about the proprietor of the *Daily Mirror*? I'll show you how concerned I am – as soon as you're off this phone I'm away to the golf course."

Mr Sanderson added, "I shall be going to Mexico for the World Cup finals even if it means driving my own Mercedes to get there and you can say that while I'm there, I'll be smoking a cigar larger than Captain Bob's."

The result of the publication of the article was somewhat predictable. On his return from Seville, Sanderson was ordered to report to the MGN Manchester office. Sensing what was to happen, he engaged the services of Jock Brown, a lawyer with Ballantyne & Copland but also at the time a football commentator for STV, having been the replacement of Arthur Montford. Sanderson went down to the Manchester office and was informed that he was fired by MGN for gross misconduct. He was handed a letter on his arrival at the Manchester office stating this fact, and no appeal procedure was to be allowed.

The pent-up frustration of events at MGN had inevitably ended in the parting of ways between Sanderson and Robert Maxwell. Maxwell had reportedly been furious at Sanderson's outspoken public attacks. However it would be well into the future when Maxwell's dramatic come-uppance would occur.

Sanderson, seething with anger, was determined not to let the matter rest there. He wanted his day in court and instructed Jock Brown to prepare a case for unfair dismissal to be heard by an industrial tribunal, knowing that it would create unwanted publicity for Robert Maxwell and MGN. He was aware his chances of victory were extremely slim, and that even if he won the case on the grounds of no appeal being allowed by MGN, that he would be found to have contributed significantly to his dismissal by his behaviour.

As it transpired, the case for unfair dismissal was heard in December 1985 in Glasgow, not long after the death of Jock Stein. However, drama had unfolded shortly before as Sanderson had himself suffered a heart attack and was in the intensive care unit of the Victoria Infirmary on Glasgow's south side. The tribunal panel wanted to hear the case at a future later date, but Jock Brown was instructed by Sanderson's wife Sheila just to get the case over with. She had been concerned at the stress that the Maxwell events had caused her husband. Since being dismissed in March 1985 Sanderson had lost the mainstay of his earnings, although Radio Clyde work and appearances on STV had shored him up, along with a column for the *Evening Times*. He had been bailed out to some extent by his colleague of many years Alex Cameron of the *Daily Record*, in that Alex Cameron had suggested that Sanderson should be appointed press officer for the Edinburgh Commonwealth Games in 1986 given his vast experience of press events. This post was based in Canning Street, Edinburgh, and put an added strain on Sanderson's health.

Sanderson lost his case for unfair dismissal, as well as an appeal. It was determined that he had "bitten the hand that had fed him" by the tribunal panel. He had not been fit to attend the hearing, which took place in his absence as he resided in a hospital bed. He had no choice but to recuperate at home for three months. He was no longer on the airwaves during this period from December 1985 to February 1986.

Ironically this would not be the end of his dealings with Maxwell. By a quirk of fate, the one year contract he had taken as press officer for the Commonwealth games in Edinburgh from early 1985, after being fired from MGN, once again would expose him to difficult circumstances. This was because the Commonwealth Games organising committee was now in terrible financial trouble, and had appealed for a 'White Knight' who could offer financial assistance. Robert Maxwell answered their call.

One of the many stories reporting Robert Maxwell's antics while being associated with the Commonwealth Games in 1986 comes from the Derek Bateman and Derek Douglas book. They tell the tale of Maxwell attempting to sack Sanderson for a second time, this time from his fixed-term press officer position. Maxwell, on being informed by a group of members of the Scottish press that Sanderson was once again in his employ, had then quickly announced:

> "So far as I'm concerned Mr Sanderson is a former employee and is now the former press officer. I have sent him a letter. I hope he has received it."

In fact no such letter had ever been sent and some behind-the-scenes discussions later that day (not involving Sanderson) led the whole episode being dropped. On hearing the events and comments from Maxwell, Sanderson had told reporters Bateman and Douglas: "I've handled bigger fish than Maxwell in my time. . . "

Robert Maxwell would later achieve notoriety, having plundered the Mirror Group Newspapers pension fund, stealing over £400 million from it (Source: *Enquiry by the Department of Trade & Industry Report on Mirror Group Newspapers plc, 2001).* Maxwell died on November 5th, 1991, in mysterious circumstances, having apparently fallen overboard from his luxury yacht. His business empire had collapsed.

Sanderson's comments back in 1985 in the *Evening Times* had largely been proved correct. Maxwell was not as successful in his business dealings as the majority of people had thought. The money stolen from the MGN pension fund had been used to shore up his empire, which eventually came crashing down due to massive levels of debt.

Back in early 1986, Sanderson had convalesced from his heart attack, and was ready for his come-back on Radio Clyde. Gerry McNee, Hugh Keevins and Chick Young had covered the slot in his absence and had done well.

Sanderson's return was warmly greeted by callers and listeners. He was not a particularly well man at this point, and he was instructed by doctors that he was not to travel to the World Cup finals in Mexico to be held later that summer.

However, he was now something of a celebrity in Scottish football. He had appeared on stage with Ian St John and Jimmy Greaves (then phenomenally successful with their ITV programme 'Saint & Greavsie') as part of a Radio Clyde Football Road-show with Richard Park. On the announcement of his name by Paul Cooney as he sat on the stage, he was met with boos and hisses from the audience, similar to the treatment that a villain in a pantomime show would receive.

"Good, at least it means that you are listening to what I have to say!" retorted Sanderson cheekily to the crowd; the response being met with good-natured laughter and applause. Tom Shields, the *Herald* columnist, told the tale of a company who approached comedian and impressionist Allan Stewart with regard to impersonating Sanderson's voice for a radio advert. The price quoted for this service from Stewart was £200. Shields then explained that the company decided to approach Sanderson himself, who did the job for £50.

Sanderson's outspoken views would eventually and inevitably upset a prominent Premier League manager. The *Evening Times* reported events under the headline: 'Why Fergie's in a Huff – Scots Boss won't appear on TV with Jimmy Sanderson'.

The *Evening Times* story read:

Controversial Evening Times columnist James

Sanderson has withdrawn from BBC TV's SuperScot quiz show. This is because Aberdeen manager Alex Ferguson would not appear with him. Mr Sanderson said that despite signing a contract to appear he has agreed not to because Mr Ferguson said he would not appear on the programme with him

But Mr Sanderson said today: "I am not chickening out, I am doing what I think to be the gentlemanly thing to avoid any embarrassment for anyone. It's not me who would have been embarrassed."

Mr Sanderson said that 'embarrassed' BBC bosses had phoned him at home to put Mr Ferguson's views. The programme, which will be televised on Scottish Cup Final day, is being recorded in Glasgow on Sunday.

Mr Sanderson said: "Mr Ferguson seems to think I am too critical in my writing and on my radio broadcasts. I reserve the right to give my opinion."

Alex Ferguson said today: "James Sanderson does not concern me, I am not getting involved in that."

Disc jockey Tom Ferrie has been drafted in as a late substitute for the panel, along with Hearts chairman Wallace Mercer, comic Andy Cameron and Alex Ferguson.

(Evening Times, May 2nd, 1986)

In late 1986 Alex Ferguson headed down to Old Trafford to embark on what has become a phenomenally successful career as manager of Manchester United spanning over twenty years. Scotland was now perhaps too limiting for his talents, and the 'big stage' beckoned.

On the announcement that Alex Ferguson was leaving Aberdeen to go to Manchester United, Sanderson was interviewed by Jim White on STV about Ferguson's departure:

James Sanderson: "I don't think we should be weeping and wailing about Alex Ferguson going, Jim. It was time for him to go. I think it's a good thing for Aberdeen that he is going at long last, because I think his ambitions lay elsewhere; and we are very fortunate that we've got so many bright men able to step in and do a good job."

Jim White: "It's fair to say that there is no love lost between yourself and Ferguson, James?"

James Sanderson: "Well he just didn't speak to me, but I don't mind that. He'll find the wolves in Manchester to be much worse than I was, I'm sure."

Ferguson's managerial achievements at Manchester United would make him one of the most highly regarded managers in the world, and of course he would become *Sir* Alex Ferguson following Manchester United's victory in the UEFA Champions League in 1999, where his team would come from behind in dramatic fashion and snatch victory in the dying minutes, winning 2-1 against Bayern Munich.

Chapter 7: 1986 – Sanderson's Finale

1986 would prove to be a big year in Scottish football. Heart of Midlothian looked unstoppable as yet another alternative force to the Old Firm started to dominate. Hearts had developed a strong squad; with Henry Smith, Walter Kidd, Sandy Jardine, Gary MacKay, Craig Levein, John Robertson, John Colquhoun and Sandy Clark all regular picks. If Hearts could win the league title for the 1985/86 season, it would mean that there would be no Old Firm winner of the Premier League for four seasons on the trot. "The Old Firm supporters may think that they have a divine right to win games, but they are mistaken," Sanderson warned.

Following the death of Jock Stein, Scotland had qualified for the 1986 World Cup Finals in Mexico that summer. In late 1985 the Scots had won a play-off against the Oceanic group winners Australia to qualify – a 2-0 win at Hampden on 20th November with goals from Davie Cooper and Frank McAvennie was followed by a 0-0 result in the return in Melbourne on 4th December. Sanderson had not travelled to Australia because of a heart attack. Indeed, 1986 would be Sanderson's finale.

In Europe for 1985/86 Celtic had been ordered to play a 'closed doors' Cup Winners' Cup fixture against Athletico Madrid, and went out in the first round. Rangers also lost in the first round of the UEFA Cup to Osasuna. The New Firm fared better, Dundee United got to the third round of the UEFA Cup before losing to Swiss team Neuchatel Xamax, and Aberdeen managed to get to the quarter final of the European Cup, losing to IFK Goteborg. St Mirren lost to Swedes, Hammarby in the second round of the UEFA Cup.

Sanderson had returned to the airwaves on Radio Clyde in early 1986, just in time for the 1985/86 season title run-in. Celtic had slowly crept up on Hearts, who had been the league pace-setters for months and had sustained a long unbeaten run in the league. The result was a tense climax, with pressure mounting on Hearts to hold on to a diminishing lead. It would go to the final game. Hearts would play away against Dundee at Dens Park, whilst Celtic would play St Mirren at Love Street. Not only would Celtic have to win, they would need a feast of goals, and hope that Dundee could thwart Hearts. The improbable then occurred, and Celtic supporters were euphoric at the final whistle. Hearts had lost 2-0 to Dundee, courtesy of two goals from Albert Kidd in the last eight minutes, and Celtic had thrashed St Mirren 5-0. It was joy for Celtic manager Davie Hay and total misery for Hearts manager Alex MacDonald. To put the tin-lid on it, Hearts would also lose the 1986 Scottish Cup final 3-0 to Aberdeen, who had already bagged the League Cup that season.

"There is a cacophony of sound at the final whistle here at Love Street," shouted Sanderson into the microphone, barely audible above the screams of jubilation from Celtic supporters within earshot of the open-style press box in the main stand. The threat from yet another East coast club in succession (for the fourth year running) winning the Premier league title had been halted. Hearts supporters would be inconsolable for years after.

Scotland competed in the World Cup in Mexico in June 1986, with Alex Ferguson in charge as manager for the trip. Scotland were making a habit of qualifying for World Cup Finals – this was their fourth in a row from 1974, but yet again they were unable to progress to the second round.

Sanderson took part in a World Cup Road Show, organised by a major brewer. This involved watching each of the three Scotland games in a series of large hotel venues in the Glasgow area and giving opinions at half time and at the final whistle to a large audience. Bob Crampsey also took part. How Sanderson must have wished he had been deemed medically fit to travel to Mexico! However, he was Press Officer for the Commonwealth Games that same year in Edinburgh, and was committed to seeing the job through.

Scotland would lose the opener against Denmark 1-0, lose to West Germany 2-1 (with Gordon Strachan scoring a great goal from a tight angle, then being unable to jump over the back-boards in celebration), and draw a bad-tempered game 0-0 with Uruguay (who have earned notoriety as a fairly bad-tempered team). Sanderson correctly predicted on radio that Argentina would win the 1986 World Cup; he did not predict however that 'the hand of God' would be a significant factor, with Diego Maradona using a fist to send the ball past England keeper Peter Shilton in the Argentina v England match.

Earlier Scottish football had been rocked by the sensational arrival of Graeme Souness as player/manager at Ibrox in 1986, shortly before the Mexico World Cup finals in which Souness played. The events were secretive, and it was Jim White of Scottish Television that broke the story. White had earlier gone to Italy and had filmed a documentary about Souness playing at Sampdoria. Souness in turn gave White and STV the exclusive of his arrival at Rangers.

Within months of Souness's arrival, many matches at Ibrox would become all-ticket affairs. This had become necessary because of a huge upturn in attendances, often requiring the doors to be locked on pay at the gate supporters. In one match in January 1987, against the now defunct Clydebank, the gates had to be shut some twenty minutes before the kick-off for two of the stands, leaving thousands disappointed outside. Sanderson had commented on Scottish Television several months earlier: "We have wooed and won; coaxed and cajoled people back into our football grounds. Our clubs are in the middle of a bonanza."

Times were changing and the appetite of Rangers fans to watch their team was now insatiable, a complete contrast to that of around five years earlier under the management of John Greig and then later Jock Wallace, when attendances had nose-dived. The stampede for season tickets had now commenced. The 'Ibrox revolution' was now in full swing. David Murray would take financial control at Ibrox from Lawrence Marlborough in November 1988.

Over the next decade, Rangers would go on to dominate Scottish football, and emulate arch rivals Celtic in the feat of nine league championships in a row from the season of 1988/89 up to 1996/97. Souness would pursue his football management career south of the border, with Walter Smith taking the helm at Ibrox as his replacement.

On the Radio Clyde phone-in, Sanderson had been asked what he felt about Souness's appointment. He stated that, in his opinion, it was a good choice, but felt that it would take Souness a year to turn things around at Ibrox. He explained: "Souness needs to be given time, and I think it will require over a year for Souness to mould a new team together." Sanderson tipped Celtic to win the 1986-87 league title, on the back of their success of 1985-86. The forthcoming season of 1986-87 would be a long one, with 44 games now to be played in the Premier League due to an expansion from ten to twelve clubs giving an additional eight games.

With the advent of the changes at Ibrox, the inevitable question was raised on the phone-in.

Caller: "Hello, Mr Sanderson."

Sanderson: "Hello."

Caller: "I want to ask a straightforward no nonsense question, Mr Sanderson, is that okay?"

Sanderson: "Certainly. Go ahead."

Caller: "Do you think that Rangers will now sign a Catholic with Souness being here an' that?"

Sanderson: "Yes I do."

Caller: "You think that Rangers will now go out and sign a Catholic just because Graeme Souness has come to Ibrox as manager?"

Sanderson: "Yes, I am in no doubt that Graeme Souness will sign a Catholic to play for Rangers!"

It would not be immediate, but Rangers would eventually sign a Roman Catholic in due course in a blaze of publicity, namely the ex-Celtic player Mo Johnston in 1989 from French club Nantes (Rangers had a Catholic player, John Spencer, already at the club in fact). It would be another sign of progress in the Scottish game.

Sanderson had been less impressed with the choice of the new Scotland manager, Andy Roxburgh. As journalist and broadcaster Chick Young wrote at the time (with a fair measure of tongue-in- cheek):

> "Like the rest of reasonably minded people in the West of Scotland I do not see eye to eye with Mr Sanderson most of the time. For example, while I applaud the appointment of Andy Roxburgh as manager of Scotland, the little one (Sanderson) was screaming horror within seconds of the SFA announcement. But at least he speaks his mind. Sitting on the fence, in terms of voicing opinion, is a prospect which pains him as much as the physical act."
>
> (*Evening Times*, 2nd August, 1986)

Scottish football would also start to benefit from an influx of good players arriving from English clubs. There was a reason for this. English clubs had been banned from European competition in the wake of the Heysel stadium disaster at the Juventus v Liverpool European Cup Final held in Brussels in 1985. English players were viewing playing in Scotland as attractive, as Scottish clubs could participate in Europe. By joining top Scottish clubs the English players could gain European experience that had been denied to English clubs.

As always, Scottish teams and supporters were anxious when learning their fate as to who they would meet in European competition. It was always hoped a favourable draw would result, giving a tie against the weaker teams in Europe. Managers usually were cautious even if the draw was extremely favourable for their team, only to be castigated by Sanderson who, in his usual ebullient manner, pointed out:

> "Some managers complain regardless of the opposition. Some would complain if they were drawn against a pack of Girl Guides from the Faroe Islands."
> (Scottish Television interview, 1986)

In the domestic league, Sanderson's opinion that Celtic would win the Premier League title for season 1986/87 appeared to have merit, as Celtic established a fairly substantial lead early in the campaign. However, he would not witness the outcome as the season gradually unfolded.

On the morning of Saturday 6th December, 1986, Sanderson called the Radio Clyde office saying that he would not be able to commentate at the match that day. He stated that he may require a hernia operation that Monday. This was in fact knowingly untrue, as Sanderson was experiencing chest pains similar to the heart attack he had endured in December 1985. On Monday 8th December, 1986, he died at the Victoria Infirmary of a heart attack. Sanderson was gone, but the popularity of the Radio Clyde football phone-in would ensure that he would not be forgotten.

Chapter 8: The Show Must Go On

Following Sanderson's death it would be Gerry McNee on Radio Clyde who would initially follow the formula of success that had been forged on the Super-Scoreboard Open line. He would commentate on the turning point from late December 1986 and January 1987, where Celtic let slip a substantial lead and Rangers romped home as league winners for 1986/87. Rangers also won the League Cup that season.

He would also report on St Mirren winning the Scottish Cup Final against Dundee United courtesy of an Iain Ferguson goal in extra-time. Dundee United demonstrated that the New Firm still had much to offer by reaching the 1987 UEFA Cup Final over two legs against Swedes IFK Goteborg, disposing of the mighty Barcelona along the way. Although they were defeated 2-1 on aggregate, it was still irrefutable evidence that Dundee United and Aberdeen had been the Scottish representatives that had excelled in Europe in the 1980s, not the Old Firm.

It would now be Celtic's turn to experience years in the doldrums. Although winning the double in their centenary year of 1987/88; their old foes Rangers would then match the nine championships in a row record from 1988/89 to 1996/97 and dominate Scottish football. It would be Celtic's turn as a club to experience a radical revolution with the arrival of Fergus McCann, replacing the Kelly and White dynasty. As Rangers had done before them, Celtic invested in a new stadium and found money to build a stronger squad.

Following the revolution at Parkhead both Old Firm clubs had something very much in common – they now had massive numbers of season ticket holders. The armchair supporters who for years could not be enticed to see their team in the flesh on the park were now attending matches. They were now at the game in such numbers that they usually filled the capacity for Ibrox and Celtic Park (around 50,000 and 60,000 respectively), figures unthinkable some twenty years earlier. Even for what could be considered run-of-the-mill domestic games, tickets were in short supply, such was the fervour and enthusiasm of the very high proportion of season ticket holders.

These statistics in terms of sell-out games were being matched at Tynecastle, where another revolution, headed by a Lithuanian, Vladimir Romanov, resulted in dramatically increased and regular full capacity attendances of around 16,000 spectators. Time will tell if this trend will continue. The importance of financial backing for football clubs has not been better illustrated by the achievements of Gretna and their millionaire owner Brooks Mileson, when the Borders club made the final of the 2006 Scottish Cup against Hearts and took Hearts all the way to a penalty shoot-out after a 1-1 deadlock after extra time. Gretna became an SPL club in 2007. It should also not be forgotten that complying with rules for all-seated grounds for Premier League membership tested the finances of many a club (just ask those at Partick Thistle).

In Europe, the European Cup was replaced with the UEFA Champions League in the early 1990s, and the European Cup Winners' Cup competition was scrapped and instead amalgamated with the UEFA cup by the year 2000. A little known player called Bosman would serve up massive implications following a legal ruling in the European courts in 1995 that would change the way transfer dealings in particular would be agreed. Players could be sold by clubs if 'still in contract', but a player at the end of their contract would be free to move to another club in the European Union without the payment of any fee. One consequence of the Bosman ruling would be the proliferation of agents negotiating the best deals that they could for their clients. The realisation that football is a short career meant that the old adage of 'playing for the jersey' became redundant. It also produced what could be termed 'football mercenaries', playing for what they could get from their employing club, and moving on for better deals (negotiated by their agent). Stories of players from past eras are part of the motivation for this trend, fuelled by fear – i.e. show immense loyalty to one club, but end up broke when your playing days are done.

Clubs now knew that if they did not sell a player on while 'under contract', the player could leave when the contact expired, and the club would not get a penny. It may now be considered wise to 'cash-in' on a star player, even if the club supporters were against this, to bolster club finances.

The reward of three points for a win (instead of two), introduced from season 1994/95, would make draws in football a less favourable outcome for clubs, and would encourage teams to push for victory in the final minutes of matches and thus encourage attacking play. In Scotland, experimentation with end of season play-offs would become a new development for determining promotion and relegation, the aim being to engender excitement for supporters on the last day of the season.

The Scottish Football League would again experiment with reorganisation of the league, giving four divisions from 1994. Sanderson had always expressed his concerns that in terms of club voting rights "the tail was wagging the dog." Eventually the Premier Division clubs in Scotland would form a breakaway league, resigning from the Scottish Football League and forming the Scottish Premier League (SPL) from season 1998/99.

The national team would continue to qualify for World Cup Finals in both 1990 and 1998, and indeed European Championship Finals as well in 1992 and 1996, with both Andy Roxburgh and Craig Brown acquitting themselves well as managers of Scotland. As usual though, Scotland would be unable to progress past the first round. However the national team would then endure a lengthy lean spell where qualification for the finals of World Cups and European Championships would not materialise, although Berti Vogts would take Scotland to a play-off decider over two legs against the Dutch in November 2003 for the Finals of the 2004 European Championships.

At club level, Celtic would compete in a UEFA Cup final in 2003 in Seville, and narrowly lose 3-2 to Porto in extra time under the managerial leadership of Martin O'Neill. The Celtic support would be awarded the FIFA Fair Play Award for 2003.

As ever, managers continue to come and go (and in the case of Walter Smith at Ibrox, they sometimes return). Managers today now require to possess specific qualifications in the form of coaching badges, a far cry from the days of the great Bill Struth as Ibrox manager (from 1920-1954), who Sanderson had always pointed out to callers was an excellent manager ". . . who had never kicked a ball."

Perhaps a more relevant question to ask many spectators today is not "Were you at the game?" but instead, "Did you see the game?" (in line with the rapid developments in cable and satellite television that are now taking place). It remains to be seen if rising football attendances are sustainable for the Scottish game in the future, such are the difficulties for both clubs and spectators alike to balance the books. One thing is certain, the football phone-in is sure to thrive.

ESPAÑA 82

P

JAMES MILLAR
SANDERSON
G 801164
DAILY MIRROR ANDERSTON Q.
101 PERIODISTA
ESCOCIA
0609400190

Spain 1982 – the last World Cup Finals
Sanderson would attend

Were You at the Game?

References

Bateman, D. & Douglas, D. (1986) *Unfriendly Games –
    Boycotted and Broke*, Edinburgh: Mainstream Publishing

Ferrier, B. & McElroy, R., (2005) *Rangers: The Complete
    Record,* Derby: Breedon Books

MacPherson. A., (2005) *Jock Stein;* Berkshire: Highdown

Ross. D., (2005) *The Roar of the Crowd: following Scottish
    football down the years;* Glendaruel: Argyll Publishing

Shields, T., (1991) *Tom Shield's Diary;* Edinburgh:
    Mainstream Publishing

Watt, J. & Gillier N. (1981) *Watt's My Name – An
    Autobiography*; London: Stanley Paul

Were You at the Game?

Appendix

Premier League Winners

1979/80   ABERDEEN

1980/81   CELTIC

1981/82   CELTIC

1982/83   DUNDEE UNITED

1983/84   ABERDEEN

1984/85   ABERDEEN

1985/86   CELTIC

1986/87   RANGERS

Scottish Cup Winners

1979/80	CELTIC
1980/81	RANGERS
1981/82	ABERDEEN
1982/83	ABERDEEN
1983/84	ABERDEEN
1984/85	CELTIC
1985/86	ABERDEEN
1986/87	ST MIRREN

League Cup Winners

1979/80	DUNDEE UNITED
1980/81	DUNDEE UNITED
1981/82	RANGERS
1982/83	CELTIC
1983/84	RANGERS
1984/85	RANGERS
1985/86	ABERDEEN
1986/87	RANGERS

**Premier Division final positions
(seasons 1979/80 to 1986/87)**

Premier Division 1979/80 (36 games played)

	Points	Goal Diff.
1. Aberdeen	48	+32
2. Celtic	47	+23
3. St Mirren	42	+7
4. Dundee Utd	37	+13
5. Rangers	37	+4
6. Morton	36	+5
7. Partick Thistle	36	-4
8. Kilmarnock	33	-16
9. Dundee	26	-26
10. Hibernian	18	-38

(Hearts & Airdrie promoted from 1st Division)

Premier Division 1980/81 (36 games played)

	Points	Goal Diff.
1. Celtic	56	+47
2. Aberdeen	49	+35
3. Rangers	44	+28
4. St Mirren	44	+9
5. Dundee Utd	43	+24
6. Partick Thistle	30	-16
7. Airdrie	29	-19
8. Morton	28	-22
9. Kilmarnock	19	-42
10. Hearts	18	-44

(Hibernian & Dundee promoted from 1st Division)

Premier Division 1981/82 (36 games played)

	Points	Goal Diff.
1. Celtic	55	+46
2. Aberdeen	53	+42
3. Rangers	43	+12
4. Dundee Utd	40	+23
5. St Mirren	37	-3
6. Hibernian	36	-2
7. Morton	30	-23
8. Dundee	26	-26
9. Partick Thistle	22	-24
10. Airdrie	18	-45

(Motherwell & Kilmarnock promoted from 1st Division)

Premier Division 1982/83 (36 games played)

	Points	Goal Diff.
1. Dundee Utd	56	+55
2. Celtic	55	+54
3. Aberdeen	55	+52
4. Rangers	38	+11
5. St Mirren	34	-4
6. Dundee	29	-11
7. Hibernian	29	-16
8. Motherwell	27	-34
9. Morton	20	-44
10. Kilmarnock	17	-63

(St Johnstone & Hearts promoted from 1st Division)

Premier Division 1983/84 (36 games played)

	Points	Goal Diff.
1. Aberdeen	57	+57
2. Celtic	50	+39
3. Dundee Utd	47	+28
4. Rangers	42	+12
5. Hearts	36	-9
6. St Mirren	32	-4
7. Hibernian	31	-10
8. Dundee	27	-24
9. St Johnstone	23	-45
10. Motherwell	15	-44

(Morton & Dumbarton promoted from 1st Division)

Premier Division 1984/85 (36 games played)

	Points	Goal Diff.
1. Aberdeen	59	+63
2. Celtic	52	+47
3. Dundee Utd	47	+34
4. Rangers	38	+9
5. St Mirren	38	-5
6. Dundee	37	-2
7. Hearts	31	-17
8. Hibernian	27	-23
9. Dumbarton	19	-35
10. Morton	12	-71

(Motherwell & Clydebank promoted from 1st Division)

Premier Division 1985/86 (36 games played)

	Points	Goal Diff.
1. Celtic	50	+29
2. Hearts	50	+26
3. Dundee Utd	47	+28
4. Aberdeen	44	+31
5. Rangers	35	+8
6. Dundee	35	-6
7. St Mirren	31	-21
8. Hibernian	28	-14
9. Motherwell	20	-33
10. Clydebank	20	-48

(No relegation as Premier Division expanded to 12 teams for next season; Hamilton Accies & Falkirk promoted from 1st Division)

Premier Division 1986/87 (44 games played)

	Points	Goal Diff.
1. Rangers	69	+62
2. Celtic	63	+49
3. Dundee Utd	60	+30
4. Aberdeen	58	+34
5. Hearts	56	+21
6. Dundee	48	+17
7. St Mirren	36	-15
8. Motherwell	34	-21
9. Hibernian	33	-26
10. Falkirk	26	-39
11. Clydebank	24	-58
12. Hamilton Accies	21	-54

(Morton & Dunfermline Ath promoted from 1st Division)

Other books from Argyll Publishing

www.argyllpublishing.com